BEC Vantage
Masterclass
Upper Intermediate

Workbook with key

Nick Brieger

Jeremy Comfort

Nina O'Driscoll

Fiona Scott-Barrett

OXFORD
UNIVERSITY PRESS

OXFORD
UNIVERSITY PRESS

Great Clarendon Street, Oxford OX2 6DP

Oxford University Press is a department of the University of Oxford.
It furthers the University's objective of excellence in research, scholarship,
and education by publishing worldwide in

Oxford New York

Auckland Cape Town Dar es Salaam Hong Kong Karachi
Kuala Lumpur Madrid Melbourne Mexico City Nairobi
New Delhi Shanghai Taipei Toronto

With offices in

Argentina Austria Brazil Chile Czech Republic France Greece
Guatemala Hungary Italy Japan Poland Portugal Singapore
South Korea Switzerland Thailand Turkey Ukraine Vietnam

OXFORD and OXFORD ENGLISH are registered trade marks of
Oxford University Press in the UK and in certain other countries

ISBN-13: 978 0 19 453199 3

Printed in China

ACKNOWLEDGEMENTS

*The authors and publisher are grateful to those who have given permission to
reproduce the following extracts and adaptations of copyright material:*
p28 Extract from 'Work-Related Stress: A Short Guide' published by the
Health and Safety Executive. Reproduced by permission of Her Majesty's
Stationery Office.
p31 Extract from 'Health and Safety Statistics 2000/01' published by the
Health and Safety Commission. Reproduced by permission of Her Majesty's
Stationery Office.
p36 Extract from 'How to Beat the Stress Interview' by Nick Corcodilos from
www.asktheheadhunter.com. Reproduced by permission of North Bridge
Group Inc.
p60 Extract from 'Why Customer Service Fails' by Niels Kjellerup from
www.callcentres.com.au. Reproduced by permission.
p61 Extract from 'Telephone Greetings' by Mary Sandro from
www.ProEdgeSkills.com. Reproduced by permission.
p66 Fair Trade Federation Principles and Practices. Reproduced by
permission of the Fair Trade Federation www.fairtradefederation.org.

Although every effort has been made to trace and contact copyright holders
before publication, this has not been possible in some cases. We apologize
for any apparent infringement of copyright and if notified, the publisher
will be pleased to rectify any errors or omissions at the earliest opportunity.

We would like to thank the following for permission to reproduce photographs:
Anthony Blake Photo Library: p 9 Tim Imrie; Avis p 43 (CR); BackCare p 29;
Cafédirect Ltd p 66 (R); Canon p 43 (TC); Copyright of BMW AG p 43 (TL);
Corbis UK Ltd.: pp 4 Bettmann/ 6 Wild Country (T)/ 6 Jose Luis Pelaez, Inc.
(B)/ 14 Larry Williams/ 15 Jon Feingersh/ 18 Torleif Svensson/ 19 Jose Luis
Pelaez, Inc./ 37 Chuck Savage/ 39 Pawel Libera/ 50 Jon Feingersh/ 58 Della
Zuana Pascal SYGMA/ 61 Ariel Skelley/ 65 Owen Franken/ 66 Owen Franken
(L)/ 67 David Katzenstein/ 69 Jose Luis Pelaez, Inc. (L)/ 69 Hulton-Deutsch
Collection (R)/ 71 David Stoecklein/ ; Getty Images: pp 21 Stephen Derr The
Image Bank/ 22 The Image Bank/ 24 Taxi/ 45 The Image Bank/ ; Iams p 43
(TR); Ikea p 43 (BL); Linographic pp 46 (L)/ 46 (R); Microsoft Corporation p 43
(BR); Oxford University Press pp 34-35/ 48 (C)/ 48 (B)/ 48 (A)/ 48 (D)/ 48 (E)/ 48
(F)/ 48 (G)/ 48 (H)/ 48 (I)/ 48 (J)/ 59/ ; Perrier p 43 (CC); Powerstock Superstock
p 60; Rex Features: pp 54 Henryk T. Kaiser/ 73/ ; The Nescafé name and
logos reproduced with the kind permission of Société des Produits Nestlé
S.A. p43 (CL)

Illustrations by:
Mark Duffin: pp 33
Nigel Paige: pp 8, 13, 16, 28, 30, 36, 38, 40, 53, 56, 63, 68, 73

contents

unit 1 people and companies

vocabulary

1 Match the following business sectors (1–12) with the activities involved in them (a–l).

1 Automotive	a This industry produces medicinal drugs used to diagnose, detect, treat and prevent disease.
2 Aviation	b We manufacture a wide range of drinks.
3 Beverages	c Our technology transmits information over media such as telephone wires or radio waves.
4 Construction	
5 Information Technology	d This industry builds cars – from research through design to final development.
	e We supply the fuel needed by most road vehicles.
6 Media	f We design and build large buildings, roads, bridges and tunnels.
7 Mining	g This sector includes television, radio and newspapers.
8 Petroleum	h We manufacture aircraft.
9 Pharmaceuticals	i We make fibres that can be made into fabric.
10 Retail	j This industry deals with the generation, transmission, reception and storage of information.
11 Telecommunications	k This sector includes any shop that sells direct to the public.
12 Textiles	l We develop processes to extract useful minerals from the land and the seas.

2 Look at the descriptions of famous companies and match each company with the entrepreneur who started it.

Akio Morita   Henry Ford   Michael Dell   Ray Kroc   Sam Walton   Ted Turner

Henry Ford and son with Model F Ford

a This man developed the automobile, which had been invented in Europe, into an everyday form of transport in America.

b He took a single McDonald's hamburger stand and built it into a global brand.

c He helped turn Sony into a worldwide force in the electronics industry.

d He built Atlanta-based CNN and TBS into a global cable industry, now part of AOL Time Warner.

e He was the founder of Wal-Mart and Sam's Club chains.

f Two years after starting his computer business in his university bedroom, he had 250 employees. A decade after that, in 1996, he opened his on-line computer store, which today sells more than $14 million in computers and associated products a day.

3 Find fourteen words connected with work in the word-square.

R	C	H	E	U	A	C	I	O	J	N	P	W	T	A
E	V	J	G	Y	I	A	L	U	R	E	H	I	N	M
U	W	O	R	K	E	R	E	F	S	W	I	V	B	C
P	O	B	F	S	E	E	T	U	Y	U	N	K	L	R
I	E	D	S	F	R	E	E	L	A	N	C	E	W	S
C	M	V	G	E	N	R	D	F	E	M	O	F	I	K
Z	P	A	W	Y	S	C	B	I	L	I	M	P	G	I
B	L	E	C	N	E	M	P	L	O	Y	E	E	I	L
P	O	N	O	E	C	D	Y	M	L	B	H	R	O	L
G	Y	T	M	A	U	V	S	E	R	V	I	C	E	S
R	E	N	P	U	R	J	W	N	L	E	P	M	T	N
O	R	G	A	N	I	S	A	T	I	O	N	Y	I	P
S	E	F	N	U	T	O	L	S	N	J	L	C	V	M
A	F	B	Y	D	Y	R	M	A	N	A	G	E	R	W

4 learning tips

When learning new words, it is useful to learn related parts of speech. You can then keep a record of these words. Complete the table, following the example.

noun – concept	noun – people	verb	adjective	negatives
employment	employer – employee	employ	employed	unemployed – unemployment
•	•	organise	•	•
communication	•	•	•	•
•	•	•	manageable	•
•	creator	•	•	•

reading

Read the following article about types of companies. Choose the best word to fill each gap from A, B, C or D below. For each question 1–15, mark one letter (A, B, C or D).

The mixed economy

Britain is a model of a mixed economy. It is (0)........C.......... up of two (1)....................
of companies: privately-owned organisations and (2)....................-owned enterprises.
The objectives of those who (3)................... business in these two sectors are quite
different, as private sector firms are owned by individuals, and public sector firms and
organisations are owned by central or (4)................... government. Most businesses in
Britain are privately (5)................... and this sector is clearly (6)................... as a key
area of the economy. The (7)................... objective of firms in the private sector is to
(8)................... a larger share of the market. This can be (9)................... through an
(10)................... in sales. This in (11)................... will enable the business to grow, for
example, through buying up another company. The (12)................... company will then
have a greater (13)................... of entering different markets. The public sector has
different (14)..................., the principal one being to (15)................... essential services,
such as health and education.

0	A built	B grown	C made	D constructed
1	A styles	B kinds	C areas	D forms
2	A country	B state	C nation	D land
3	A perform	B make	C do	D carry
4	A restricted	B local	C narrow	D limited
5	A made	B arranged	C managed	D driven
6	A looked	B watched	C noticed	D seen
7	A main	B most	C first	D top
8	A add	B gain	C build	D expand
9	A achieved	B completed	C done	D finished
10	A addition	B enlargement	C increase	D expansion
11	A cycle	B turn	C circle	D roll
12	A larger	B greater	C fatter	D heavier
13	A try	B aim	C luck	D chance
14	A matters	B concerns	C alarms	D affairs
15	A give	B provide	C put	D find

listening

🎧 You will hear a presentation by an expert talking about the current situation and likely future trends in the world of work. For each question 1–7, mark one letter (A, B or C).

1 The speaker's presentation is based on
  A his extensive research.
  B his own views.
  C popular information.

2 The speaker says that a good education
  A is normal for everyone.
  B is normally necessary for a successful career.
  C is always necessary to succeed.

3 If employers want their employees to stay, they must
  A provide opportunities for training.
  B identify those with the potential to succeed.
  C motivate them.

4 According to the speaker, people who have worked hard
  A are helped to succeed.
  B show great virtues.
  C have strengthened the country's economy.

5 The system of rewards must provide
  A financial benefits.
  B non-financial benefits.
  C both financial and non-financial benefits.

6 According to the speaker, people who have retired should
  A take some responsibility for their own financial situation.
  B rely on the state for a state pension.
  C be aware of the nation's economy.

7 According to the speaker, organisations are
  A reducing the number of levels of management.
  B facing more competition.
  C seeing the benefits of new technology.

language in use: question forms

1 Classify the following questions into closed, open or indirect.

	question type
1 Can you explain in more detail what benefits should be guaranteed?	
2 How can employers play their part?	
3 I'd like to know how jobs are likely to change in the future.	
4 Does the future look good for the economy?	
5 Is getting and keeping a good job the sole responsibility of the employee?	
6 What should pensioners do to enjoy their retirement?	

2 Look at the following interview about the future of work and write the best question for the answers given. Write an indirect question in 3 and 5.

A (1) ....?
B They can prepare for the future by becoming more aware.

A (2) ....?
B They need to become more aware of the importance of demographic changes.

A (3) ....?
B Yes, they will certainly affect the world of work.

A (4) ....?
B In my opinion, this trend started in the 80s.

A (5) ....?
B The main changes will certainly be the disappearance of jobs for life.

A (6) ....?
B Yes, I certainly see this as an inevitable trend.

A (7) ....?
B I have specifically chosen this trend as I think it will totally change the world
  of work.

3 Interview a partner about trends in the world of work. Try to use a mix of closed, open and indirect questions.

writing

When you write a document – a memo, e-mail, fax or letter – it is important to choose the right style. One aspect of style is using the right greeting and farewell. These need to match each other and be written in the appropriate style.

Match the type of document (1–4) with the appropriate greeting (a–d). Then choose a farewell from the following list. Some farewells may be appropriate for more than one document.

Best regards	Best wishes	Bye	Regards
See you	Yours faithfully	Yours sincerely	

type of document	greeting	farewell
1 Informal e-mail to person whom you know well	a Dear Sir / Madam	
2 Letter to a person whose name you don't know	b Dear Mr Schulz	
3 Letter to person whose name you know	c Dear Jenny	
4 Letter to person whom you know well	d Hi Pete / Hello	

fun and games

Read the following famous sayings about work (1–8) and match each saying with its explanation (a–h).

1 It's not where you are today that counts. It's where you are headed.
Arthur F. Lenehan

2 A man can fail many times, but he isn't a failure until he gives up.
Anonymous

3 A manager is not a person who can do the work better than his men; he is a person who can get his men to do the work better than he can.
Fred Smith

4 Work expands so as to fill the time available for its completion.
C. Northcote Parkinson

5 Attitudes are more important than facts.
Dr. Karl Menninger

6 Choose a job you love, and you will never have to work a day in your life.
Confucius

7 A great man shows his greatness by the way he treats little men.
Thomas Carlyle

8 Adversity is the springboard to great achievement.
Anonymous

a Efficiency is about working in a better way, not about having more time.
b If you like your work, you'll enjoy your life.
c If you stop trying then you are a failure.
d There is no success without failure.
e Successful men behave in a fair way to their employees.
f The most important skill for managers is the ability to motivate their staff.
g The way you think is more important than what you know.
h Set yourself targets.

unit 2 company structure

vocabulary

1 Match the departments (1–10) with the quotes (a–j).

1 Administration

2 Finance

3 Human Resources

4 Information Technology

5 Marketing

6 Production

7 Purchasing

8 Quality

9 Research and Development

10 Sales and Distribution

a We are very dependent on technology; my job is to ensure that all the hardware and software is operational.

b I am responsible for sourcing all materials, equipment and components needed by the firm.

c My team provides detailed figures to assess the health of the company.

d The Marketing Department identifies gaps in our product range. We create the new products and then test them.

e We are concerned with manufacturing in our two factories.

f When a job becomes vacant or a new post is created, we take care of recruitment and selection.

g We work with a large team of national representatives whose job is to get orders from customers and then ensure that the orders are delivered.

h My department has a wide range of responsibilities from running the post room to organising office furniture.

i We find out what customers want, set the prices and organise promotion campaigns.

j I ensure that all our products are manufactured to the highest possible standard.

2 Look at the short description of the marketing department of IceBerg and choose the appropriate word or phrase to complete the sentences.

carries out	is headed	leads	organises	solves
deals with	in charge	manage	are responsible	supported by

IceBerg makes and sells ice cream both nationally and internationally. The marketing department (1)............................... by the Director, Johannes Fleischer. His department (2)............................... detailed market research in order to identify opportunities for new product development. Johannes (3)............................... a team of market researchers, who, in turn, (4)............................... for specific product areas. The team (5)............................... lots of reports from internal and external sources. This information is passed to Johannes, who is (6)............................... of collating the information so that it can be presented to the Board. Johannes also (7)............................... problems connected with pricing, and (8)............................... promotional campaigns for new (and old) products. In addition to the market research team, Johannes is also (9)............................... an assistant and a secretary. They (10)............................... his schedule and prepare all his appointments.

3 Medico is a competitor of Sonic NV. In the following job descriptions from Medico, some of the words have been scrambled. Rearrange the letters to complete the sentences.

MARKETING MANAGER

PRINCIPAL RESPONSIBILITIES

- Provides in-depth market, industry and (1)....................... (mcvioeptite) analysis.
- Develops pricing and packaging (2)....................... (tsiresgeta).
- Works closely with the sales (3)....................... (emta) to develop sales methods and training.
- Develops and manages (4)....................... (rmutecso) care programmes.

MARKET RESEARCH ASSISTANT

PRINCIPAL RESPONSIBILITIES

- (5)....................... (salenysa) statistical data on past sales to predict future sales.
- Attends (6)....................... (erconfeencs) and gather data on competitors.
- Prepares (7)....................... (restrop) and provide management with information needed to make decisions on promotion, distribution and pricing of products.

PRODUCT MANAGER

PRINCIPAL RESPONSIBILITIES

- Understands customer (8)....................... (desne) and market trends.
- Manages new product definition, planning and (9)....................... (nacluh) activities.
- Works closely with internal (10)....................... (posgru) and external partners.

4 learning tips

Some word combinations are based on grammatical relationships, e.g. *responsible for*; others are based on meaning relationships, e.g. *advertising campaign*. Try to learn these word combinations as units as well as individual words.

grammatical combinations	meaning combinations
carry out	product range
deal with	recruitment and selection
in charge of	to solve a problem
responsible for	advertising agencies

Match words from columns a and b to find eight word combinations.

a	b
1 department	arrangements
2 travel	control
3 market	information
4 quality	meeting
5 product	systems
6 support	research
7 team	staff
8 information	members

Read the text below about the origins of company structure. For each question 1–6, mark one letter (A, B, C or D) for the answer you choose.

WHAT ARE THE ORIGINS OF COMPANY STRUCTURE?

If we look at the structures of companies, we can see how they have reflected the current mix of ideologies at any one time: political, social, legal and economic, to mention but four. On the other hand, we can also say that structure is a normal feature of human nature. In other words we prefer organisation to chaos and we respond well to clearly defined areas of activity. In this way we can see in the earliest communities the beginnings of organisational structure.

If we look for the practical applications of this thinking, a good starting point is the Ford Motor Company. Henry Ford, who set up his automobile manufacturing company in 1903, firmly believed that efficiency in the workplace was based on providing just that mix of knowledge and skills required to carry out a single, often repetitive, task. Therefore the training provided to his workers focused on what was needed to do the job.

Today, companies structured according to this approach would be considered very minimalist, since they are only concerned with narrow areas of competence. Modern management has had to pay much more attention to the needs of the workforce and find ways to motivate them. Today's worker is not only a unit of production, but also a resource with clearly defined needs and wants. This, in turn, has had implications for companies in the way they structure and organise their activities. This move to a more human face came at a time of rapid industrial change and gave the workers a new position in the company hierarchy. In addition, management began to change, moving away from more autocratic models, where a single leader has total power, to broader ones involving a greater degree of power-sharing. This breadth was reflected in the particular mix of skills needed for success. These can be summarised as:

- planning what needs to be done
- leading the team of colleagues and workers who are going to do it
- organising the work in the most efficient manner
- controlling what has been done to ensure that it meets the plan.

These four areas have remained the cornerstone of management. While companies may have changed their hierarchies and become leaner and flatter, the tasks carried out by managers have remained largely unchanged. The Marketing Manager needs to prepare the marketing plan, in terms of activities and budgets; then he or she needs to ensure that the plan is communicated to all those who are to be involved in its implementation; after this stage comes the implementation itself and the manager needs to organise the work of those who are to carry it out; and finally, to complete the process, the results need to be compared against the plan. What we have stated for the Marketing Manager is repeated throughout the company, with minor adaptations to fit each department's activities and concerns.

1 Company structures are based on
A four principles.
B more than four principles.
C human nature.
D primitive societies.

2 According to the author, people like to
A live in a well-ordered society.
B work together on shared tasks.
C have a degree of risk in their lives.
D work in clearly defined organisations.

3 Henry Ford provided
A wide-ranging training for his workers.
B very repetitive training for his workers.
C beliefs and visions for his workers.
D narrowly focused training for his workers.

4 Today's workers
A are simply tools of production.
B have lower expectations than their predecessors.
C have recognisable requirements and wishes.
D are more efficient than their predecessors.

5 According to the author, successful managers need
A to exercise a range of skills.
B to be good at planning tasks.
C to lead by example.
D to follow models from well-established companies.

6 Why does the author give marketing as an example?
A because it is a typical management area
B because it is a unique management area
C because marketing is central to all company structures
D because companies today are marketing-driven

listening

🎧 KTP is a medium-sized engineering company which makes components for the motor industry. You will hear a presentation by their Managing Director, talking about the changes he is planning for the company and its structure. For each question 1–7, mark one letter (A, B or C) for the correct answer.

1 The speaker is giving the presentation because
A the volume of business is due to rise next year.
B the volume of business has risen recently.
C the volume of business has fallen recently.

2 The speaker says that their company hierarchy
A is appropriate for the market.
B is not appropriate for the market.
C needs minor changes to respond to the market.

3 The speaker says that a flatter structure is needed
A in sales.
B in sales and purchasing.
C throughout the company.

4 The speaker intends to improve
A contacts with suppliers.
B the procedures for paper-based purchasing.
C the procedures for on-line purchasing.

5 In finance, the newly appointed controller will
A work with Greg Barnes.
B replace Greg Barnes immediately.
C check Greg Barnes' work.

6 The speaker would like the IT department to
A control the business.
B take over the functions of purchasing.
C support the other departments in the company.

7 The main purpose of the proposed new team is to
A share information on ways of working.
B study the use of computer media.
C arrange information meetings.

language in use: present simple and present continuous

1 Classify the following sentences into:
- present simple for usual activities and routines (PS1)
- present simple for general or permanent situations (PS2)
- present continuous for current or temporary activities (PC1)
- present continuous for definite arrangements in the future (PC2)

1 The Marketing Director heads the national and international marketing team.	
2 At present he is planning to buy companies in Eastern Europe.	
3 IceBerg review the marketing plans in the six-monthly marketing meetings.	
4 At these meetings the country managers present the results in their markets.	
5 Next year IceBerg are moving their European headquarters to Brussels.	
6 They are starting a new sales campaign in the autumn.	

2 Complete the following extract from a presentation, using either the present simple or the present continuous of the verb in brackets.

We normally (1)........................... (review) our company structure in the light of market developments. This (2)........................... (not always involve) making changes, but it always (3)........................... (lead) to a fruitful discussion. So, what (4)........................... (the current situation show)? At present we (5)........................... (experience) a change in emphasis – away from markets to products. This (6)........................... (mean) more emphasis on diversifying the product range. In our current structure, each business unit (7)........................... (have) its own structure and each director (8)........................... (report) to the Managing Director. This structure (9)........................... (work) well in those markets where the business is separate. At present we (10)........................... (notice) a move towards integration. So, we (11)........................... (plan) to change our company structure accordingly. I (12)........................... (not foresee) any major changes for the next six months as these developments (13)........................... (not normally happen) overnight. However, I (14)........................... (expect) further feedback by the time of our next meeting. I am sure that we all (15)........................... (share) the same vision for this company.

writing

The following memos sent by the personnel department about new appointments have got jumbled up. Match the beginnings (1–4) with the correct endings (a–d) to produce four memos.

MEMO 1

TO   all sales staff

FROM   personnel department

RE   <u>appointment of new Sales Manager</u>

We are pleased to announce that as of 1 September, Jos de Witt will take over from Mark Mardel.

MEMO 2

TO   Finance Director

FROM   personnel department

RE   <u>confidential appointment</u>

This is to let you know that the new controller will start on 1 September.

MEMO 3

TO   all admin personnel

FROM   personnel department

RE   <u>admin issues</u>

I am pleased to announce that the re-organisation of the mail room is now complete.

MEMO 4

TO   Factory Manager

FROM   personnel department

RE   <u>update on appointment</u>

This is to let you know that Michael Merrick has now got back to us.

a He has confirmed that he is happy to take up the job of night shift supervisor.

b His key responsibilities will be to obtain customer orders from our reps and ensure delivery.

c Mandy Stein has agreed to take on the key role of supervisor. We hope you will all give her your support.

d According to the information that you have provided, he will work on key budgetary issues until the end of the year.

fun and games

Read the following story and answer the questions below.

A new manager spends a week at his new office with the manager he is replacing. On the last day the departing manager tells him, 'I have left three numbered envelopes in the desk drawer. Open an envelope if you face a crisis you can't solve.'

Three months later there is a major crisis, everything goes wrong and the manager doesn't know what to do. He remembers the parting of his predecessor and opens the first envelope. The message inside says 'Blame your predecessor!' He does this and gets out of the difficult situation.

About six months later, the company is experiencing a collapse in sales, together with serious product problems. The manager quickly opens the second envelope. The message reads 'Reorganise!' This he does, and the company quickly recovers.

The following year, at his next crisis, he opens the third envelope. The message inside says 'Prepare three envelopes.'

1 What does *predecessor* mean?

2 What happens to the manager?

unit 3 business travel

vocabulary

1 Match each of the business travel locations (1–8) with the most appropriate phrase (a–h).

1	business class cabin	a	Could you bring me the wine list, please?
2	airline check-in desk	b	Could I have a gin and tonic, please?
3	bar	c	Could you take me to this address, please?
4	hotel reception	d	Good afternoon, madam, which main course would you like from the in-flight menu?
5	meeting room	e	This is the smaller room. It'll easily accommodate twelve delegates.
6	restaurant	f	Yes, Mrs Rankine. I've got your reservation here. Could you fill in the registration form, please?
7	conference venue	g	I'd like a window seat, please.
8	taxi	h	We reserved a stand by the main entrance.

2 Look at the exchanges from business travel dialogues and choose the appropriate word or phrase to complete the sentences.

aisle	check in	hand luggage	reservation	ticket
book	excess baggage	receipt	seat belt	tip

1 A Checking in for Tokyo? Could I see your .... and your passport, please?
   B Yes, here you are.

2 A Should I leave something for the waiter?
   B Service is actually included in the bill, but you can leave a small ...., if you like.

3 A Where do I .... for New York?
   B Let me just see your ticket. Right, madam. At desk 11 or 12.

4 A We're about to take off. Could you fasten your ...., please?
   B Yes, of course.

5 A Here's your American Express card, sir, and your ....
   B Thanks very much.

6 A I'm afraid you are only permitted 20 kg.
   B How much will the .... charge be?

7 A Could you put your .... either under your seat or in the overhead locker?
   B Could you help me, please?

8 A Would you like a window or .... seat, sir?
   B Window, please.

9 A I'd like to make a .... for a double room for the weekend of 1 November.
   B One moment, madam. I'll just check if we have one available.

10 A If you .... a Class B car, we'll upgrade you to a Class A free of charge.
   B Well, if it's free, why not.

3 Match words or phrases from columns a and b to find eight word combinations connected with business travel.

a	b
a frequent	economy
b overnight	seat
c time	flight
d health	flyer
e global	of the job
f jet	lag
g a perk	risk
h cramped	zone

4 learning tips

Nouns combine with other words to form various different patterns:
- adjective + noun, e.g. *frequent flyer*
- noun + noun, e.g. *jet lag*
- noun + prepositional phrase, e.g. *a perk of the job*

Match the remaining phrases from exercise 3 with these patterns.

language in use: comparatives and superlatives

1 Some of the following sentences contain mistakes. If a sentence is incorrect, make the necessary corrections.

1 A hotel suite is usually much bigger than a double room.
2 Book as early as possibly to get the best seat.
3 Air tickets are now sold by supply and demand: the greater the demand for tickets, the higher the prices.
4 I'm afraid that your luggage is heavier than the permitted weight.
5 If you want to get to the city centre, public transport is much more quicker than a taxi in the rush hour.
6 Teleconferencing is much convenient than travelling to overseas meetings.
7 The few tired you are, the more efficient you'll be in the meeting.
8 The most simple precaution is to cover your health by suitable insurance.

2 Look at the statement made by a business traveller, and complete the text using the comparative or superlative form of the words in brackets.

These days I find that air travel is much (1).............................. (hard) than a few years ago. Queues seem (2)............................ (long) and journeys are (3)............................
.... (time-consuming). In fact, I think that air travel has not made the world (4)............................ (small). There is evidence that journey times are (5)............................ .... (slow) as they were 25 years ago. And comfort hasn't improved either. London has some of (6)............................
.... (expensive) hotels I have ever seen. You get (7)............................ (little) and (8)............................ (little) for your money. Unless you belong to the super-executive class, London offers you (9)............................
.... (bad) value for money of any European city. That's my opinion.

3 Interview a partner about their experiences of personal and business travel. Try to use the vocabulary from this unit and as many comparative and superlative forms as possible.

reading

Look at the statements below and the advertisements for products for business travellers. Which product (A, B, C or D) does each statement 1–7 refer to? For each statement 1–7, mark one letter (A, B, C or D). You will need to use some of the letters more than once.

Example

0 One of my hobbies is collecting old clocks. So, when I'm travelling I like to take photos of buildings like town halls, railway stations and other historic buildings. *C*

1 As a regular flyer on long haul flights, I want something to help me fall asleep, something to help me forget the time.

2 As I always travel with my laptop, I wish I could listen to my favourite music with better sound quality.

3 I am a great believer in alternative medicine. I am looking for a way to help me cope with the effects of long haul travel, but with a non-drug based approach.

4 I need a device which can give me the time and the date in major cities throughout the world.

5 I often find myself in interesting places. When I have a couple of hours to spare, there's nothing I like more than visiting places of local interest. I often wish that I could capture the sights and sounds unobtrusively.

6 I regularly fly between time zones. I would like to know what the precise time is at any point during my journey, so that I don't feel such a big 'time jump' when I arrive.

7 People talking and cabin staff serving passengers can really disturb me. I'd like something that can block out the sound so that I can relax.

A SPEAK-UP is a totally unique inflatable speaker and headphone system. Simply pump up, plug in, and turn on to get great stereo sound from a great looking design. As the sound is projected around the total surface area of the inflatable shape, this is the only true 'surround sound' speaker system. They are compatible with PCs, Macs, personal CD players, personal stereos and MP3 players. The headphones feature a futuristic design and are the last word in comfort.

B WORLD TRAVEL CALENDAR is the perfect travel companion. Flip open the case of this travel alarm clock and you'll find an alarm clock, a calendar and a calculator. Press the calculator buttons to scroll through the time in 60 major cities, from Paris to Hong Kong. What's more, it features a 100-year monthly calendar that spans the entire 21st century.

C THE MINICAM may be smaller than a matchbox but it can still hold its own in the world of digital cameras. Capable of snapping and storing up to 80 photographs at a time, the Minicam is small enough to fit into a pocket, purse or wallet. What's more, the miniature camera can also take short digital video clips and comes with powerful image editing software.

D JET LAG ELIMINATOR is a kit containing a disk and instruction booklet. Follow the instructions and, using acupressure techniques, stimulate specific points on your body every two hours of your flight. Then sit back, relax, and enjoy the journey.

listening

🎧 Jane Ronson is making travel arrangements for her boss. You will hear three telephone conversations or messages. Write one or two words or a number in the numbered spaces on the notes or forms below.

Call 1 (Questions 1–4)
Look at the notes below. You will hear a message about vaccinations needed for travelling.

POSTING TO EAST AFRICA	Vaccinations	
	Required/Recommended	Clinics
(1)...........................	Required	Monday and (2)........................... afternoons
Typhoid	Recommended	No clinic at present; call 01205 (3)...........................
Tetanus	Recommended	Tuesday mornings
Polio	Recommended for long-term travellers	Clinics held (4)........................... in Southampton Row
Cholera	Not recommended	

Call 2 (Questions 5–8)
Look at the notes below. You will hear a message about travel insurance.

INTERINSURE AGENT NOTES	
Caller	Jane Ronson
Policy no.	(5)...........................
Comments	Change Dell to Toshiba (6)...........................
	Change winter sports cover from (7)........................... only to worldwide
Actions	Send claim (8)...........................

Call 3 (Questions 9–12)
Look at the form below. You will hear Jane phoning about lost luggage.

AIRSEARCH LUGGAGE TRACKING	
Passenger name	Dirk (9)...........................
Flight No	(10)...........................
First flight	Madrid to Amsterdam
Second flight	Amsterdam to (11)...........................
Number of items	(12)...........................

writing

Look at the extracts from four letters about business travel. In each letter, some phrases are missing. Choose from the phrases below to complete each text.

a As a regular customer, I expect to receive at least an apology for the treatment I received.
b As soon as we receive these details, we will be able to settle your claim.
c As we have received these details, we will be able to settle your claim.
d I am writing about your reservation for a Class B car.
e I am writing to complain about the service provided at your hotel on 24 March.
f My staff have informed me about the problem you experienced in your recent visit to the hotel.
g I'm sure it won't happen again.
h Thank you for informing us about the accident you had last week.
i Please quote your existing booking number when you arrive.
j I apologise for the confusion and would like to offer you free use of the facilities on your next visit.

1

Dear Sir/Madam

........f........ I understand that you had booked a meeting room but one wasn't available when you arrived. ....

2

Dear Ms Anapopoulou

.... We regret to inform you that we cannot process your insurance claim at present as we require further details. ....

3

Dear Sir/Madam

.... When I tried to check in, the queue of waiting guests stretched from the lobby into the restaurant. The whole procedure took 45 minutes. ....

4

Dear Mr Viala
.... We are pleased to be able to offer you an upgrade at no extra cost. We are sure that having a bigger car will make your journeys more comfortable and enjoyable. ....

fun and games

Are you an international traveller? Check your knowledge with these questions.

1 Where would you find Mount Kilimanjaro?
2 Of which countries is SAS the national airline?
3 Where would you find the Giant's Causeway?
4 What is the capital of Iceland?
5 In which city would you find the tiny statue called Manneken Pis?
6 What is the first language of Morocco?
7 If you were given your change in zloty, in which country would you be?
8 In which US state would you find San Francisco?
9 How many hours' time difference are there between London and Tokyo?
10 In which country is the original Raffles Hotel?

unit 4 company results

vocabulary

1 Complete the gaps in the following statement by a company chairman, presenting the end-of-year results.

bankruptcies	generated	profits	redundancies
collapse	improvement	raise	review
cutting	increase	reduce	staff

'In this brief presentation I would like to (1).......................... our results over the last year. In general it has been a tough year. We have seen a number of high profile (2).......................... in our sector. In contrast, we have managed to (3).......................... the level of (4).......................... . This has been achieved by (5).......................... our operating costs in a number of areas. Our main focus in this area has been to (6).......................... the number of (7).......................... in those regions where the economy is in danger of (8).......................... . In fact, the sale of our shops in some of these areas has (9).......................... extra income at an important time. After our programme of (10).......................... our headcount now stands at 3,589 employees. This means that we are in a strong position for the coming year, when we hope to see an (11).......................... in trading conditions and an (12).......................... in economic activity.'

2 Match the phrases of cause 1–8 with the results a–h.

1	slowdown in consumer spending	a	will push many companies into debt
2	increased High Street spending	b	will provide opportunities for expansion
3	lower marketing budget	c	will mean less TV advertising
4	no funding from banks	d	will result in redundancy programme
5	company collapse	e	has led to lower turnover
6	higher interest rates	f	means certain bankruptcy
7	increased profit	g	is likely to push up profits

3 Complete the following crossword. All the words can be found in the article on page 32 of the Course Book.

Across
- 4 other companies in the same sector (11)
- 5 shop or store which sells to the end user (8)
- 9 benefit (9)
- 11 decrease in economic activity (8)
- 12 introduce a new product on the market (6)

Down
- 1 hopeful (10)
- 2 almost the same (7)
- 3 went into, joined (7)
- 6 opposite of *success* (7)
- 7 range (7)
- 8 opposite of *interesting* (6)
- 10 found all over the world (6)

4 learning tips

Notice the adjective endings in the following words.

ful	(i)al	ive	able
successful	controversial	active	fashionable
powerful	global	aggressive	profitable

Change the following words into adjectives by using one of the above endings. You may have to make other changes to the word.

beauty	include
attract	industry
option	value
remark	express
harm	compete

Remit is an IT solutions company. In their end-of-year report, addressed to the staff of the company, the chairman gives an overview of the company's activities during the financial period and prospects for the future. Read the report. Choose the best sentence from below to fill each of the gaps. For each gap 1–5, mark one letter (A–G). Do not use any letter more than once.

Another good year for Remit

I am pleased to report that Remit has again produced an excellent set of results; the income generated in the last six months is equal to the turnover for the whole of the last financial year. (0) ....G.... Demand for our software and solutions has remained strong. A major development was that during the period Meblamet signed a contract to use our software. In addition, our business with existing customers has grown positively. In particular I would like to mention the launch of a major project for DiverSolutions. This is running according to schedule and is progressing extremely well. Our recently signed partnership with Lightings Inc is also proving effective and is clearly helping them to develop their sales.

As a result of the contract signed with DiverSolutions earlier this year, our customer base now includes seven out of the top ten life insurance companies. First Call, one of the leading independent advisors, has integrated our software into their sales administration system. (1) .... Errors are now down from 20% to 9%. In fact, they are well on the way to their target of 1%.

As announced in our preliminary results in March this year, we have increased investment in new products. As a result, an Internet-based version of our software was completed during the period. (2) .... We have already received a number of enquiries for this new adaptation which, we hope, will lead to orders during the next period.

Our strategy of designing software and solutions which help our customers to reduce costs when acquiring new business will continue. We believe there are significant opportunities for us to increase our market share by working with partners to deliver complete solutions to customers. (3) ....

The economic circumstances remain challenging. However, we remain confident about the prospects for the business. With our customer base, our original technology and healthy prospects, we have a sound base from which to continue our strong growth. In the US, the slowdown in the economy is likely to affect our rate of growth. (4) .... In addition, the Directors will ensure that costs are carefully controlled so that our profitability is not affected. We are certain that our strategy for the region is sound.

In conclusion, this has been another highly successful year for Remit in extremely demanding markets. We have continued to increase our turnover, while adding to our customer base; and, most importantly, we have kept costs under control. (5) ....

A The results have been impressive, with significant gains in accuracy and speed.

B However, at this stage this market represents a very small proportion of our total income.

C This will both extend the market for our software and create openings for new projects.

D Our customers need to respond to an increasingly competitive environment.

E This is now ready for use in the software developed for the North American market.

F We anticipate significant progress in the coming year with an improved cash position, a growing customer base and increasing turnover from new sectors.

G This is a significant achievement, particularly against a background of a general slowdown in spending and economic uncertainty.

listening

🎧 You will hear the introduction to a company's Annual General Meeting, at which the company results are presented. For each question 1–6, mark one letter (A, B or C) for the correct answer.

1 The Chairman
   A will stay in her post for five more years.
   B will soon leave the Board.
   C has just been appointed to the Board.

2 The participants of the meeting
   A have received the agenda in advance.
   B will receive the agenda at the start of the meeting.
   C got the agenda at the last meeting.

3 The end-of-year Profit and Loss statement
   A includes the results for the company's global activities, including Asia.
   B includes the results for the company's European operations.
   C includes the results for the company's global activities, excluding Asia.

4 The total number of people at the meeting who are able to vote is
   A 50.
   B 453.
   C 64.

5 The AGM needs to
   A appoint two new members for the Board.
   B consider seven candidates for the Board.
   C choose a new Chairman for the Board.

6 Zapata and Merribel
   A have prepared the accounts for the first time.
   B will be re-appointed.
   C prepare the accounts every year.

language in use: past simple and present perfect

1 Some of the following sentences contain mistakes. If a sentence is incorrect, make the necessary corrections.

   a At the beginning of the meeting the Chairman presented the agenda.
   b How long do you use Zapata and Merribel as your accountants?
   c This year's results show that the company made an unexpected profit.
   d Operating costs have decreased substantially since the summer.
   e When have you revised the budget?

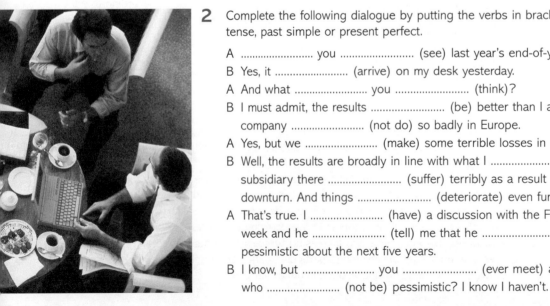

2 Complete the following dialogue by putting the verbs in brackets into the correct tense, past simple or present perfect.

   A .... you .... (see) last year's end-of-year report yet?
   B Yes, it .... (arrive) on my desk yesterday.
   A And what .... you .... (think)?
   B I must admit, the results .... (be) better than I anticipated. The company .... (not do) so badly in Europe.
   A Yes, but we .... (make) some terrible losses in South America.
   B Well, the results are broadly in line with what I .... (expect). The subsidiary there .... (suffer) terribly as a result of the economic downturn. And things .... (deteriorate) even further recently.
   A That's true. I .... (have) a discussion with the Finance Director last week and he .... (tell) me that he .... (feel) really pessimistic about the next five years.
   B I know, but .... you .... (ever meet) a Finance Director who .... (not be) pessimistic? I know I haven't.

3   Interview a partner about the financial situation in your company or the economic situation in your country. Talk about what has happened in the recent past and what happened at definite points in the past. Use a combination of past simple and present perfect forms.

writing

Jungle Joe's is a children's indoor activity centre in Dublin. In your role as Manager of the centre, you produce a regular quarterly report on sales for the key members of staff. In your report you comment on:

- the monthly sales.
- comparisons with the previous year.
- the quarter's profit.

Look at the figures below and your handwritten comments. Then, using all these notes, write your report. Write 120–140 words.

	Sales (€)			Quarter's profit (€)
	January	February	March	
This year	75,432	52,814	74,958	24,675
Last year	70,161	68,004	71,384	25,340

Sales

Jan: good increase on last year; very cold weather, lots of visitors
Feb: poor figures; Playland – new competitor offered special
          discounts; general downturn in consumer spending
March: good increase on last year, but just below target

Profit

two good months, but disappointing results; high costs – poor actual
profit; review all forecast costs before next quarter – make savings

fun and games

You have just attended the AGM of Portal Inc., the Internet Service Provider. You have started to write up your report from the notes you made. Write the report in full by changing the abbreviations in the text below.

The AGM was held on 24 September. After the Chairman presented the agenda, he asked if there was AOB.

During the meeting, the Chairman presented the P&L statement for Q1. It showed that while sales had risen to $1.4m, costs had risen by approx. 5%. The result was a very poor ROI. The Chairman said he didn't expect the biz. to improve next year.

When the CFO announced that the company would not be paying out a dividend, the shareholders demanded an explanation. There were angry scenes when it was announced that the directors had received pay rises of about 10% p.a. for the last six years.

unit 5 communication at work

vocabulary

1 Complete the sentences with the appropriate word or phrase from the list below.

e-mail	face-to-face	fax	in-house magazine	post
meeting	memo	noticeboard	office gossip	

1 I plan to send the agenda of our forthcoming meeting to all participants as an
.... attachment this afternoon.

2 Listening in to .... at the coffee machine is a good way to find out
what is really happening in the department.

3 I would prefer to discuss this departmental problem in a .... meeting.

4 As soon as the contract has been signed, I'll send it to you by registered
....

5 We are just checking the technical drawings now. We'll send them to you by
.... tomorrow morning.

6 Have you circulated the agenda for next week's .... yet?

7 We like to print letters from the company's employees in our ....,
which comes out every month.

8 You can find information about our health and safety regulations on the
.... in the corridor.

9 I'll send you a .... later with the main points from our meeting.

2 Complete the following word table.

noun	verb	adjective
1 advice		
2		confidential
3		private
4 response		
5	revolutionise	
6		sensitive
7		urgent
8	use	

3 Match a word from 1–6 with a suitable word from a–f to make a phrase related to the paperless office. Then, classify your word combinations as noun + noun or adjective + noun.

1	computer	a	arrival
2	fax	b	documents
3	imminent	c	machine
4	important	d	office
5	invaluable	e	screen
6	paperless	f	tool

4 Use appropriate phrases from exercise 3 to complete the text about e-mail.

E-mail has become an (1).............................. for business communication, replacing other forms of office communication such as the (2)............................. Of course, e-mail has its disadvantages. Many of us have experienced the feeling of staring helplessly at the (3)............................. after sending a message to the wrong person. Another drawback is that e-mail is not a very secure medium for sending (4)............................. . However, the (5)............................. of more secure systems may bring the (6)............................. a step closer.

5 learning tips

Nouns can be classified in different groups.

common nouns		proper nouns
countable	uncountable	
message	advice	Richard Metcalf

Now classify the following nouns.

correspondence	document	Microsoft	office	Wednesday
cyberspace	Mexico	network	staff	

countable	uncountable	proper

reading

Read the text below about workplace communication. In most of the lines there is one extra word. It is either grammatically incorrect or does not fit in with the meaning of the text. If a line is correct, write CORRECT. If there is an extra word in the line, write it in CAPITAL LETTERS.

A guide to good communication

0	Many employees complain about the lack of effective communication in which their	*WHICH*
00	organisations. In addition, research shows that ineffective communication often results in	*CORRECT*
01	lower productivity, and makes employees want to leave for their jobs. Therefore	....
02	we have been prepared the following brief guidelines on different channels of	....
03	communication and some tips on their use. The written communication is necessary if you	....
04	want your reader to have a permanent record of your message. However, if you should	....
05	remember that written communication is not always read as soon as it is received. Memos	....
06	and e-mails can be easily overlooked at or delayed for later consumption. So, if your	....
07	information needs immediate action, don't use this medium. When you preparing a longer,	....
08	written document, outline the key points before you write out the first draft. Then write	....
09	short notes before composing your full text. At the next stage, review it careful with the	....
10	intention of reducing down the word count by 25 per cent. Proof-read the final version	....
11	before sending it off. E-mail can be an excellent means of follow-up, so as to ensure	....
12	correct understanding of the next steps after a meeting. When you write an e-mail or a	....
	memo, write a brief, clear reference to your topic in the 'Subject' field.	

listening

1 ⌒ You will hear five extracts involving different types of communication in the workplace. For each recording, decide which type of communication is taking place. Write one letter (A–H) next to the number of the recording. Do not use any letter more than once.

1 ....   A Staff meeting
2 ....   B One-to-one meeting
3 ....   C Annual General Meeting with shareholders
4 ....   D Phone enquiry
5 ....   E Presentation
                  F Negotiation
                  G Social communication
                  H Job interview

2 ⌒ You will hear five more extracts of communication in the workplace. For each recording, decide which channel of communication the speaker(s) decide(s) to use for the follow-up step. Write one letter (A–H) next to the number of the recording. Do not use any letter more than once.

1 ....   A Presentation
2 ....   B Meeting
3 ....   C Memo
4 ....   D E-mail
5 ....   E Phone call
                  F Report
                  G Company intranet
                  H Letter

language in use: countable and uncountable nouns

1 Classify the following nouns as countable (C) or uncountable (U).

noun	type	noun	type
agenda		information	
benefit		memo	
client		report	
confidentiality		research	
machine		turnover	
gossip		work	

2 Make any corrections to the following e-mail that are necessary to make it more grammatically correct.

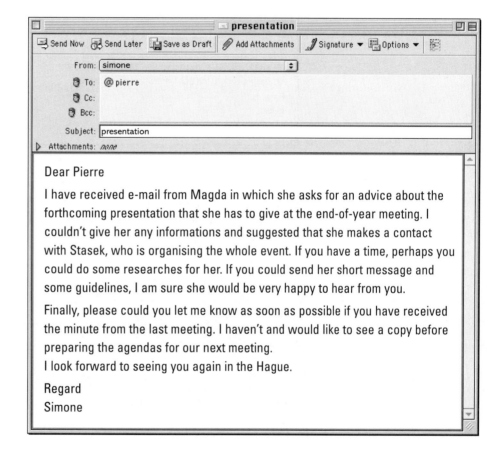

Dear Pierre

I have received e-mail from Magda in which she asks for an advice about the forthcoming presentation that she has to give at the end-of-year meeting. I couldn't give her any informations and suggested that she makes a contact with Stasek, who is organising the whole event. If you have a time, perhaps you could do some researches for her. If you could send her short message and some guidelines, I am sure she would be very happy to hear from you.

Finally, please could you let me know as soon as possible if you have received the minute from the last meeting. I haven't and would like to see a copy before preparing the agendas for our next meeting.
I look forward to seeing you again in the Hague.

Regard
Simone

writing

Read the exam tasks below and rewrite the e-mails to improve the style and vocabulary choice. Remember to check that the word count is correct. (You only count the words in the actual message.)

1 Peter Brown is the store manager of GlobalComputers, a retailer of PC equipment in Brentwood. He has ordered some PCs from his distribution centre in Brussels, which have not arrived yet.

Write an e-mail of 40–50 words to Monica de Vries, the Customer Relations Manager:
* pointing out that the order (IF435) was made six weeks ago and promised within four weeks.
* saying that he urgently needs to supply the customers.
* asking her to supply a delivery date.

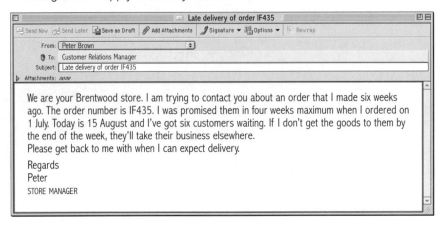

Late delivery of order IF435

Send Now | Send Later | Save as Draft | Add Attachments | Signature ▾ | Options ▾ | Rewrap

From: Peter Brown
To: Customer Relations Manager
Subject: Late delivery of order IF435
Attachments: *none*

We are your Brentwood store. I am trying to contact you about an order that I made six weeks ago. The order number is IF435. I was promised them in four weeks maximum when I ordered on 1 July. Today is 15 August and I've got six customers waiting. If I don't get the goods to them by the end of the week, they'll take their business elsewhere.
Please get back to me with when I can expect delivery.

Regards
Peter
STORE MANAGER

2 Write a reply of 40–50 words from Monica to Peter:
* apologising for the late delivery.
* explaining that there is a problem with the suppliers.
* saying that you will give him a new delivery date as soon as you have one.

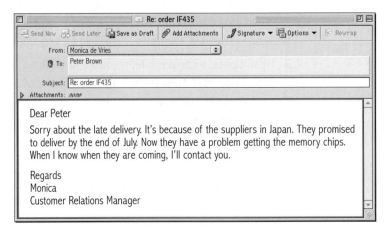

Re: order IF435

Send Now | Send Later | Save as Draft | Add Attachments | Signature ▾ | Options ▾ | Rewrap

From: Monica de Vries
To: Peter Brown
Subject: Re: order IF435
Attachments: *none*

Dear Peter

Sorry about the late delivery. It's because of the suppliers in Japan. They promised to deliver by the end of July. Now they have a problem getting the memory chips. When I know when they are coming, I'll contact you.

Regards
Monica
Customer Relations Manager

fun and games

People can communicate a great deal of information just through their body language. For example, people with arms folded, legs crossed and bodies turned away are signalling that they are rejecting messages. People showing open hands, fully facing you and with both feet planted on the ground are accepting them. What messages do you think these people are giving out?

unit 6 health and safety

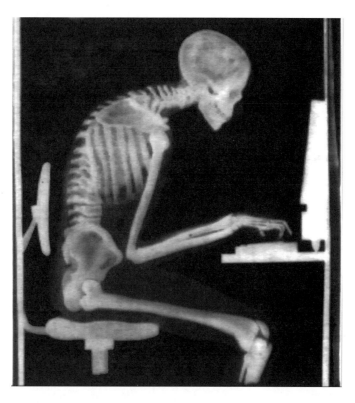

vocabulary

1 Match the following health and safety risks (1–9) with their possible consequences (a–i).

1 inadequate lighting	a risk of tripping
2 obstruction	b difficulty of escape in an emergency
3 inadequate ventilation	c repetitive strain injury
4 damaged floor surface	d eye strain
5 wet floor surface	e breathing problems
6 unsuitable furniture	f backache or other muscle pain
7 noisy equipment	g tiredness
8 prolonged work at a keyboard	h risk of slipping
9 long working hours	i damage or injury to ears

2 Complete the sentences by forming a new word from the word given in brackets. Follow the example.

a Employers must ....*comply*........... (compliance) with health and safety rules.

b Any equipment, if not maintained, can .... (danger) employees' lives.

c Tough penalties are imposed on those companies that do not observe the .... (legislate).

d Laboratory technicians must wear .... (protect) clothing.

e An .... (adjust) chair can help to prevent back and neckache.

f Employers must .... (sure) that all corridors are well lit.

g All the .... (machine) in our factory is protected by guard rails.

h .... (long) periods in front of a screen can lead to eye strain.

i Please report .... (slip) floors to the supervisor immediately.

3 Find twelve terms connected with health and safety in the following word-square.

M	V	T	A	D	J	U	S	T	A	B	L	E	T	A
F	H	J	G	Y	I	S	M	V	T	E	I	J	H	M
V	A	D	R	O	Z	O	N	E	S	N	E	V	J	C
Q	Z	B	F	S	E	B	U	V	Z	T	M	F	B	S
J	A	D	S	F	R	S	E	L	I	N	S	L	I	P
D	R	A	D	I	A	T	I	O	N	M	L	F	I	O
A	D	B	C	U	T	R	B	A	J	S	I	P	G	I
S	M	E	S	N	E	U	P	L	U	Y	P	E	I	G
A	P	N	T	E	C	C	Y	T	R	I	P	R	O	L
F	Y	T	R	A	U	T	S	E	Y	V	E	C	E	S
E	N	D	A	N	G	E	R	N	L	E	R	M	T	N
T	R	G	I	O	J	D	B	S	J	N	Y	V	I	P
Y	F	E	N	V	S	P	M	T	O	K	M	D	W	N

4 learning tips

Notice the following verb + particle phrases: *dispose of, switch off*.
In some phrases, the particle is a preposition and the noun follows the particle:
Dispose of the container carefully.
In others, it is an adverb and the following noun can often be placed either before or
after the particle: *Switch off all equipment after use*, or *Switch all equipment off after use*

Label the particles in the following sentences as prepositions (P) or adverbs (A).

a Corridors must be unobstructed to allow people to move **around** the office.
b Put **on** protective gloves when handling chemicals.
c An employer may have to pay **for** your glasses.
d Prolonged use of a mouse may result **in** repetitive strain injury.
e You must comply **with** the regulations.
f Wash **out** all containers after use.
g You may ask **for** an eye test.

reading

Read the following guidelines to employers about stress in the workplace. For each question 1–6, mark one letter (A, B, C or D) for the answer you choose.

Stress in the workplace

What is stress?

Stress is the adverse reaction people have to excessive pressure. It isn't a disease. But if stress is intense and goes on for some time, it can lead to mental and physical ill health (e.g. depression, nervous breakdown, heart disease). Being under pressure can often improve performance, but when demands and pressures become excessive, they lead to stress. And it's clear from the recognised symptoms of stress that it's actually bad for you.

As an employer, is it my concern?

Yes. It's your duty in law to make sure that your employees aren't made ill by their work. And stress can make your employees ill. Also, action to reduce stress can be very cost-effective. The costs of stress to your organisation may show up as high staff turnover, an increase in sickness absence, reduced work performance, poor timekeeping and more customer complaints. Stress in one person can also lead to stress in staff who have to cover for their colleague. Also, employers who don't take stress seriously may leave themselves open to compensation claims from employees who have suffered ill health from work-related stress.

Under health and safety law, what must I do about stress?

Where stress caused or made worse by work could lead to ill health, you must assess the risk. A risk assessment for stress involves:

- looking for pressures at work that could cause high and long-lasting levels of stress
- deciding who might be harmed by these pressures
- deciding whether you are doing enough to prevent that harm.

If necessary, you must then take reasonable steps to deal with those pressures.

Isn't stress also caused by problems outside work? Are you saying I have to do something about that?

You're not under a legal duty to prevent ill health caused by stress due to problems outside work (e.g. financial or domestic worries). But non-work problems can make it difficult for people to cope with the pressures of work, and their performance at work might suffer. So being understanding to staff in this position would be in your interests.

Are some people more likely to suffer from stress than others?

We're all vulnerable to stress, depending on the pressure we're under at any given time: even people who are usually very hardy. As an employer, you're responsible for making sure that work doesn't make your employees ill. If you notice that someone is particularly vulnerable because of their circumstances, look at how their work is organised. See if there are ways to relieve the pressures so that they do not become excessive. However, unless you know otherwise, you can assume that all your employees are mentally capable of withstanding reasonable pressure from work.

How do I recognise stress in a particular person?

Many of the outward signs of stress in individuals should be noticeable to managers and colleagues. Look in particular for changes in a person's mood or behaviour, such as deteriorating relationships with colleagues, irritability, indecisiveness, absenteeism or reduced performance. Those suffering from stress may also smoke or drink alcohol more than usual or even turn to drugs. They might also complain about their health: for example, they may get frequent headaches.

1 According to the first paragraph, the guide states that
   A both stress and pressure produce bad reactions.
   B there is a link between stress and other illnesses.
   C stress can help you to do better.
   D depression is caused by pressure.

2 Why is it important for employers to take stress seriously?
   A The law requires them to make their workplaces stress-free.
   B Reducing stress can be very expensive.
   C Ignoring stress in employees may be expensive for the organisation.
   D Stressed workers complain a lot.

3 According to the law, employers must
   A make sure that all pressures are removed.
   B implement immediate procedures to reduce stress.
   C analyse the causes of illness in the workplace.
   D carry out a study to identify work-related stress.

4 According to the fourth paragraph, the guide states that
   A employers are not obliged to deal with non-work related health problems.
   B employers must be aware of their employees' home situations.
   C stress at work may influence an employee's home life.
   D employees need to be aware of the causes of stress.

5 In the fifth paragraph, the guide states that employers
   A must ensure that employees don't fall ill because of their job.
   B should organise their work carefully.
   C can help employees by reorganising their work.
   D mustn't think that every employee can put up with stress.

6 An employer may know when employees are under stress because
   A they will give a warning signal.
   B the outward signs are always visible.
   C consumption of cigarettes may increase.
   D they are always unhappy.

listening

🎧 You will hear an interview with a Health and Safety expert, talking about workplace accidents. For each question 1–8, mark one letter (A, B, or C) for the correct answer.

1 The basis for calculations is
A fatal and non-fatal accidents.
B accidents per 100,000 workers.
C accidents per 1,000 workers.

2 The rate for non-fatal accidents is
A 648.1 per 100,000 workers.
B 295 per 100,000 workers.
C lower than fatal accidents.

3 Compared to the previous year, the number of fatal accidents
A was 75 lower.
B was 295 higher.
C went up.

4 During the 90s the rate of fatal injury to workers
A increased.
B decreased.
C was statistically significant.

5 The trend for non-fatal accidents during the 90s shows
A a decrease.
B a stable figure.
C a decrease followed by a constant rate.

6 A comparison between the sexes shows that
A men in work are at greater risk than women for all types of accidents.
B men are at greater risk than women for fatal accidents.
C men working in industry are at greater risk than women.

7 In terms of age, the statistics show that
A young workers are at a higher risk.
B older men are at a higher risk of less serious injury.
C the risk of non-fatal accidents is the same for younger and older workers.

8 Risks of workplace accidents are decreased if
A workers are given proper training.
B a worker's questions are answered.
C a worker is employed for fewer hours per week.

language in use: modals

1 Modal verbs can typically express a range of meanings, some of which are shown below. Complete the table with the following meanings.

| ability | inability/impossibility | possibility/permission | prohibition |
| advice | obligation | prediction when there is doubt | |

modal	meanings
can	
can't	
could	
may	
must	
mustn't	
should	

2 Complete the dialogue between a health and safety inspector and a factory manager with an appropriate modal verb.

A I'm afraid that at this stage we (1).................. give you a health and safety certificate.

B I realise that there are some problems. So, what specific areas of risk (2)................. we concentrate on?

A In my opinion, there are various risk areas that (3).................. be corrected. Firstly, the lighting (4)................... be upgraded. At present it may cause eye strain to workers who spend long hours on the factory floor.

B Yes, we (5)................. certainly improve the lighting. No problem with that.

A Secondly, as we were going round, we noticed a number of wet floor surfaces. These (6).................. cause someone to slip and to injure themselves. We therefore recommend a regular inspection of all floors.

B Fine. I've made a note of that.

A A third area of concern is the noise coming from the factory equipment. At present this is acceptable, but the company (7)................... let the noise level increase any further.

B We realise that this is a problem and are planning to invest in new equipment. (8)................... I just ask if you think that these improvements will solve our problems?

3 Discuss with a partner any health and safety improvements that can, should or must be carried out at his / her workplace.

writing

When writing a document, it is important not only to use the right language, but also to choose the correct style. Below is a brief report written by Miroslav Cernik, who had an accident at his workplace. Look through the report and make any necessary improvements to the language and style.

> **ACCIDENT REPORT FOR HEALTH AND SAFETY DEPARTMENT**
>
> Hello. I'm Miroslav Cernik. I am a car body sprayer. I work in the paint shop. More than five years now.
>   It was on 14 January at 11.30, in the paint workshop. I had an accident. I was carrying materials to my workplace. Then I fell on the floor. The floor was wet. And slippery. I went to the company nurse. She treated my arm. She said, 'It's broken. You must go home.' I am off work now. More than one week. I am unable to help at home. I go to the physiotherapist every day. She treats me.
>   Please look at my claim very soon.

fun and games

1 The following signs are prohibitions in the workplace. What can't you do when you see each of these signs?

2 The following signs refer to emergencies in the workplace. What does each sign refer to?

unit 7 recruitment and training

vocabulary

1 Match the following recruitment terms (1–10) with their definitions (a–j).

1 candidate	a document that a candidate completes and sends to a prospective employer
2 hire	b decision-makers who conduct an interview
3 interview	c an unfilled job
4 job application	d certificates and diplomas that someone has gained
5 qualifications	e document which gives information about a person's suitability for a job
6 recruitment agency	f to choose someone for a job
7 reference	g meeting at which someone is asked questions to decide whether they are suitable for a job
8 selection board	h to reduce the applications to a smaller number of candidates, who are to be invited for interview
9 shortlist	i organisation that matches job candidates with employers
10 vacancy	j person who applies for a job

2 Marcus Westerberg is a programmer with five years' experience of working for an international bank. He has decided to look for a new job. Put the following stages from his job-hunting process into the correct order. The first one has been done as an example.

a He is invited for interview. ....

b He identifies a suitable position. ....

c He waits for the results of the interview. ....

d He requests a detailed job description. ....

e He signs a contract of employment. ....

f Marcus looks through the job ads. ....

g He answers the interviewers' questions. ....

h He is offered the job. ....

i He discusses the financial package. ....

j He writes a letter of application. ....

3 Complete the crossword. All the words can be found in the article on page 56 of the Course Book.

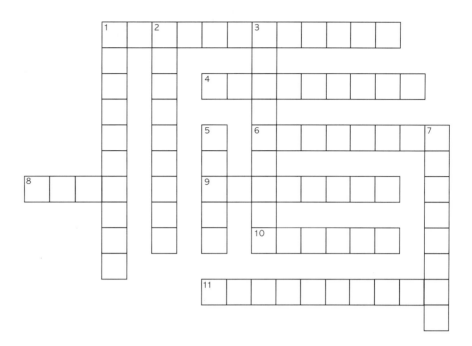

Across

1 Before you apply for a position, ensure that you satisfy the job .... (12)
4 Specialist .... is required to do certain jobs. (9)
6 vacancies (8)
8 When the job applications arrive, the first task is to .... through them. (4)
9 Recruitment .... specialise in finding suitable candidates for vacant positions. (8)
10 special abilities (6)
11 Well-designed job advertisements are good for .... the right candidates. (7)

Down

1 people in an organisation who specialise in running job interviews (10)
2 'Only candidates who are suitably .... should apply.' (9)
3 'We hope to persuade potential new .... that our company is the one to join.' (9)
5 A job .... is an Internet site which lists vacant positions. (6)
7 this occurs when there is not enough of something (8)

4 learning tips

Notice how numbers are expressed.
- $400–$500: four hundred to five hundred dollars (specific numbers)
- there are hundreds of these job boards (not a specific number)
- thousands of companies are experimenting with electronic recruitment (not a specific number)

Some of the following sentences contain mistakes. If a sentence is incorrect, make the necessary corrections.

a Employees can choose from more than fifty training courses.
b Each year we recruit about hundred and twenty new employees.
c Of course we receive literally thousands of letters from applicants.
d Management salaries start at between forty and fifty thousands dollar.
e More than a million of units come off the production line each year.

reading

Dealing with interviews and interviewers can be stressful. Read the following extract from guidelines for handling interviews. In most of the lines there is one extra word. It is either grammatically incorrect or does not fit in with the meaning of the text. If a line is correct, write CORRECT. If there is an extra word in the line, write it in CAPITAL LETTERS.

How to beat the stress interview

O	Stress interviews are still common in many companies. A stress interview is where the	*CORRECT*
OO	employer lines up a bunch of interviewers (one at a same time or all together) whose mission	*SAME*
01	is to intimidate you. The purpose of this interview: to find out how you handle the	....
02	stress. If you find yourself facing to several interviewers who stare at you intently, or	....
03	who fire questions at a rude, rapid pace while someone watches at your every move	....
04	(waiting to see what your body language will reveals), you need to take control of the	....
05	interview. The best way to deal with such interviews is to ask for an interview agenda in	....
06	advance. Who will attend the interview? What are their jobs? Who will be decide whether	....
07	to hire you? These are all total reasonable questions. After all, you're investing your time,	....
08	and you want to know who you're going to meet. Next, don't try to perform. Be by	....
09	yourself. Pretend you're in a department meeting and it's your turn to talk about your work.	....
10	If they try to stress you on purpose, make it yourself slow down and speak calmly and	....
11	softly. Forget about the people in the room. Remember that what matters is not even their	....
12	questions, but the quality of your answers. If you can remain calm under the pressure, you	....
	will have a good chance of making a good impression on the interviewer.	

---

listening

🎧 Global Training has developed a concept that brings together companies that need to train their employees and skilled trainers who can deliver the training. You will hear Fabiella di Ponte, the company's CEO, talking about the services that they offer. For each question 1–8, mark one letter (A, B or C) for the correct answer.

1 When Fabiella began her training career
  A she worked freelance.
  B she was employed by a company.
  C she acted as an external consultant.

2 In Fabiella's opinion, training is
  A a competitive activity.
  B necessary to give employees information.
  C one of the keys to achieving one's potential.

3 Global Training's principal activity is
  A to provide training courses.
  B to select trainers.
  C to help clients find facilities for running training courses.

4 Global Training's business
   A is only aimed at professional organisations.
   B is partly generated from outside the business world.
   C mostly comes from schools and colleges.

5 Global Training organises its training courses
   A into 50 areas.
   B in 15 categories.
   C using less than 50 headings.

6 After the course objectives and content are agreed, Global Training will
   A discuss the specific requirements with the client.
   B set up the computer based training.
   C look for an appropriate trainer.

7 If the client doesn't have rooms to run the training, Global Training can
   A organise a meeting to discuss requirements.
   B identify an appropriate place for the event.
   C provide their own conference facilities.

8 Global Training recently organised
   A a conference for their own sales staff.
   B an event for one of their big customers.
   C a five-day language training course.

language in use: connectors of contrast and addition

1 Classify the following into 'connectors of contrast' (C) or 'connectors of addition' (A).

also	however	on the other hand	moreover	too	while
although	in addition	not only ... but also	though	whereas	

2 In the following text the connectors of contrast and addition are missing. Complete the sentences by choosing the more suitable word or phrase in brackets.

Rapid changes in the labour market challenge organisations (1)...............................
(not only / also) to implement winning strategies (2).............................. (on the other
hand / but also) to develop and keep talented employees. (3)..............................
(Although / However) it is vital to offer training, this may not be immediately available
and employees (4).............................. (though / also) need to feel empowered in their
present positions. (5).............................. (While / Whereas) the right training at the right
time can provide big benefits for the employer, organisations need to make certain that
their training is delivered in the right way. (6).............................. (Too / In addition),
employers need to decide whether training is the best solution to the problem.
(7).............................. (Moreover / Whereas) some employees can benefit from a training
opportunity, others may not have the temperament or talent for their current position
and no amount of training will change that. Once you've decided on training and
informed the training department, inform the trainee, (8).............................. (too / on the
other hand). Make sure they know what is expected of them. (9)..............................
(Though / In addition) this may be obvious to you, it may be less than transparent to the
prospective trainee. (10).............................. (However / Moreover) the trainee may see
the training as criticism. If, (11).............................. (on the other hand / although), you
explain the targets and procedures, this can reduce worry and improve the outcome.

writing

1 OPR, a large multinational organisation, recently set up a project team to investigate training solutions for the company. Look at the extracts 1–10 below from their report. Match the extracts with the section headings a–d.

a Purpose of the report
b Methodology
c Results
d Recommendations

1 Firstly, to gather information via interviews with training organisations and analysis of their documentation.

2 In addition, until a more thorough study has been completed, it was not considered appropriate to recommend any of the training providers.

3 Secondly, to identify relevant training organisations, particularly those leading to certificates of achievement.

4 In small teams to collect information from bodies which issue certificates.

5 In general, we found that many of the organisations lacked the necessary standards to ensure quality training.

6 The team focussed on two main objectives:

7 The project team felt that additional work needed to be done to evaluate the training programmes.

8 The aim of the report was to determine how training organisations working with new technology could improve the skill levels of OPR staff.

9 The project team members worked in the following ways:

10 Individually to assess the training organisations.

2 Put the extracts (1–10) in exercise 1 in the correct order to form the report.

fun and games

Look at the list of tips for a successful job interview and rank them.

+++ very important
++   important
+   quite important
x   not necessary

the keys to success

1 Arrive on time.

2 Introduce yourself in a courteous manner.

3 Read company materials while you wait.

4 Have a firm handshake.

5 Remove any jewellery before the interview.

6 Think about the worst question you can face in an interview.

7 Listen attentively during the interview.

8 Use body language to show interest.

9 Before the interview, find out about key people in the organisation, major products or services, size in terms of sales and employees.

10 Smile, nod and give other non-verbal feedback to the interviewer.

11 Ask about the next step in the process.

12 Thank the interviewer.

13 Write a thank-you letter to anyone you have spoken to.

unit 8 advertising and promotion

vocabulary

1 Choose the best word a, b or c to complete the following sentences.

1 We have made a little money by persuading customers to have .... ads on the website.
   a display   b banner   c full-page

2 Our business-to-business products need to be advertised in .... magazines.
   a consumer   b trade   c in-house

3 We are going to launch the product with an intensive .... campaign in the shops.
   a mailing   b Web-marketing   c point-of-sale

4 We'll be using billboards throughout the city as the main thrust of our .... advertising campaign.
   a outdoor   b media   c print

5 We need to .... ads in all the mass consumer magazines.
   a set   b place   c create

6 To promote our product, I have booked several .... on the local radio station.
   a ads   b slots   c times

7 They know what features they are looking for. It's just a question of our products standing out from the ....
   a competition   b advertisers   c consumers.

8 We want them to go out and try our product so that is why we're offering a .... which they can cut out and use.
   a discount   b reply card   c coupon

2 Complete the word family table.

noun – concept	noun – people	verb	adjective	negative
competition				
advertising				
commerce				
attraction				
appeal				
consumption				
desirability				

3 Use words from the table in exercise 2 to complete the text. The first letter of each missing word has been given.

Advertising Strategy: Shock Shampoo

We have hired an agency to develop a campaign for us. What we're looking for is an association with a.......................... people who communicate d.......................... .
At the moment our c.......................... are targeting c.......................... at the bottom end of the market. We want to a.......................... to a more upmarket buyer. We feel the way to achieve this is through print a.......................... in high-class magazines.

4 Complete the sentences with the following words.

actual	convinced	endorsement	half-page	mass	print	single
agency	display	full-page	listing	potential	series	

1 We are planning to place a .... of ads over the next few months.

2 It's not so important whether the ad is .... or .... It's more important whether it's at the front or the back, rather than the middle.

3 .... ads only work for very specific products. If you want to reach a .... market, you'll need to run them repeatedly.

4 The question is whether the consumer is going to be .... by an ad which is so unusual.

5 The ad depended heavily on the .... of major sports stars.

6 We need to decide whether to go for a simple .... or pay extra for a .... ad in the yellow pages.

7 Turning .... consumers into .... purchasers is always difficult.

8 The .... thinks we should target a wider audience using a large-scale .... ad campaign in major magazines.

5 learning tips

When you learn a new word, always learn which other words it combines with.

Example *target*

target audience/target buyers/target group (noun + noun)
e.g. *to reach your target audience*
to target an audience/to target a ... market (verb)
targeted marketing (adjective)

List combinations you can make with these words: *image, market, advertise.*

language in use: future forms

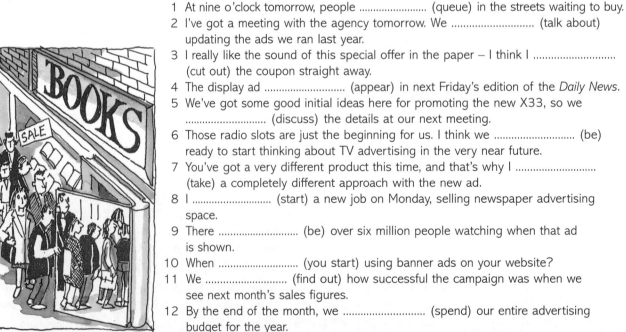

Complete the sentences with the appropriate future form of the verb in brackets.

1 At nine o'clock tomorrow, people .... (queue) in the streets waiting to buy.

2 I've got a meeting with the agency tomorrow. We .... (talk about) updating the ads we ran last year.

3 I really like the sound of this special offer in the paper – I think I .... (cut out) the coupon straight away.

4 The display ad .... (appear) in next Friday's edition of the *Daily News*.

5 We've got some good initial ideas here for promoting the new X33, so we .... (discuss) the details at our next meeting.

6 Those radio slots are just the beginning for us. I think we .... (be) ready to start thinking about TV advertising in the very near future.

7 You've got a very different product this time, and that's why I .... (take) a completely different approach with the new ad.

8 I .... (start) a new job on Monday, selling newspaper advertising space.

9 There .... (be) over six million people watching when that ad is shown.

10 When .... (you start) using banner ads on your website?

11 We .... (find out) how successful the campaign was when we see next month's sales figures.

12 By the end of the month, we .... (spend) our entire advertising budget for the year.

Read the direct mail letter below from a company which provides professional training. Choose the best word to fill each gap from A, B, C or D below. For each question 1–15, mark one letter (A, B, C or D).

P R O T R A I N   I N T E R N A T I O N A L

28 Harbour View
Sydney
Australia
e-mail: enquiry@protrain.au
www.protrain.com

Dear Ms Katelin

We are very pleased to (0).......C.......... the launch of our new programme of professional training. As you will see from the enclosed (1).................. , we have extended the range of courses considerably while (2).................. the very high quality of course design and delivery.

Above all I would like to (3).................. your attention to a suite of courses aimed at internationalising your management team. Our (4).................. course in this area is *Breaking into overseas markets*, a three-day programme (5).................. at newly appointed export managers. Alongside this course, we are also (6).................. a two-day programme on *Communicating your message internationally* and a half-day introductory workshop on *Handling foreign agents*. All these programmes have been devised (7).................. extensive research into the (8).................. of dynamic Australian companies like yours. For this reason, you can feel (9).................. that the investment in both time and money will be rewarded with (10).................. business overseas.

Protrain International has maintained its policy of (11).................. pricing. You will find some very (12).................. deals including:
• two for the price of one delegate on our winter programme.
• evening in-house training at discount (13).................. .
• major reductions on quantity bookings.

All our courses are available on both an open and in-house basis. In-house programmes can be (14).................. to suit your needs.

Please do not (15).................. to contact me and my team if you have any queries.

Yours sincerely

Shaun Kenna

SHAUN KENNA, MARKETING MANAGER

0	A tell	B describe	C announce	D sell
1	A listing	B catalogue	C record	D schedule
2	A holding	B protecting	C maintaining	D delivering
3	A draw	B hold	C pay	D keep
4	A prime	B main	C premier	D dominant
5	A fired	B sent	C aimed	D delivered
6	A giving	B offering	C promising	D rewarding
7	A following	B resulting	C preceding	D causing
8	A desires	B necessities	C needs	D urges
9	A right	B safe	C definite	D sure
10	A increased	B extra	C added	D improved
11	A sensitive	B competitive	C low	D cheap
12	A irresistible	B demanding	C attractive	D desirable
13	A fares	B penalties	C costs	D prices
14	A programmed	B designed	C cut	D guided
15	A stop	B hesitate	C trouble	D bother

listening

🎧 You will hear three telephone conversations or messages. Write one or two words or a number in the numbered spaces on the notes or forms below.

Conversation 1 (Questions 1–4)
Look at the form below. You will hear a message about placing an ad on a telephone answering machine.

CLASSIFIED ADS	
Name	Geoffrey (1)...........................
Tel No	Home: 01456 768891
	(2)......................... : 0861 3557884
Publication date	(3).........................
Ad Category	(4).........................

Conversation 2 (questions 5–8)
Look at the notes below. You will hear a woman calling about placing an ad.

Message	
Message for	David Miles
From	(5)...................... and Advertising Dept.
Re	Call from Sally Jacobs concerning advertising a property in (6).........................
Action	Call back tel no: 020 (7)......................... Please call her back this (8).........................

Conversation 3 (Questions 9–12)
Look at the notes below. You will hear a man calling about a mistake in an ad.

CLASSIFIED ADS CORRECTIONS		
Customer	Manfred Becker	
Date	Thursday 18 May	
Section	(9).........................	
Text	Customer (10).........................	Assistant
Correction	Customer (11).........................	Assistant
Action	Run free ad next (12).........................	

writing

You are the Advertising Manager for *The Great Outdoors*, a monthly walking magazine. You have received a letter from a French company who want to advertise in the magazine. They have requested information about your readership and advertising rates. Use appropriate information to complete the reply.

> 21 Guy Road
> Manchester
> MU49 5DP
>
> Dear Ms Berlot
>
> .... for your recent .... in our monthly magazine *The Great Outdoors*.
>
> *The Great Outdoors* is one of the UK's most popular walking magazines and .... the enclosed readership figures, it .... a high percentage of the UK market. I .... :
>
> • a current .... of the magazine.
> • an advertising .... card.
> The .... copy for the next issue is 5 June.
> Please .... if .... information.
>
> Yours ....
>
> *D Cartwright*
> ADVERTISING MANAGER

fun and games

It is not always obvious from a slogan what product or service is being advertised. Match the slogan (1–8) with the product (a–h) and the brand (A–H).

1 The Ultimate Driving Machine
2 We try harder
3 Technology for the environment
4 Enter the bubble
5 One thing leads to another
6 Great people with great values
7 Good for today, good for life
8 Affordable solutions for better living

a car rental
b coffee
c furniture
d mineral water
e photocopiers
f cars
g computer software
h dog and cat food

A
B **Canon**
C
D **NESCAFÉ**
E
F **AVIS**
G
H **Microsoft**

unit 9 international business

vocabulary

1 Match the words which have the same or similar meanings.

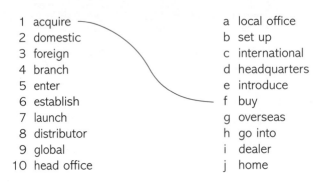

1 acquire   a local office
2 domestic   b set up
3 foreign   c international
4 branch   d headquarters
5 enter   e introduce
6 establish   f buy
7 launch   g overseas
8 distributor   h go into
9 global   i dealer
10 head office   j home

2 Complete the crossword. Most of the words are in exercise 1. The first one has been done as an example

Across

1 a local company, 51% or more owned by the parent company (10)

3 home, as opposed to foreign (8)

4 foreign (8)

7 world-wide, international (6)

8 to purchase or acquire (3)

9 to introduce a product onto a market (6)

11 site of parent company (12)

12 go into a market (5)

Down

2 a company which sells or delivers products in local markets (11)

5 establish or start a business or project (3, 2)

6 a person or company that distributes your product (6)

10 a person or company who represents your business in a local market (5)

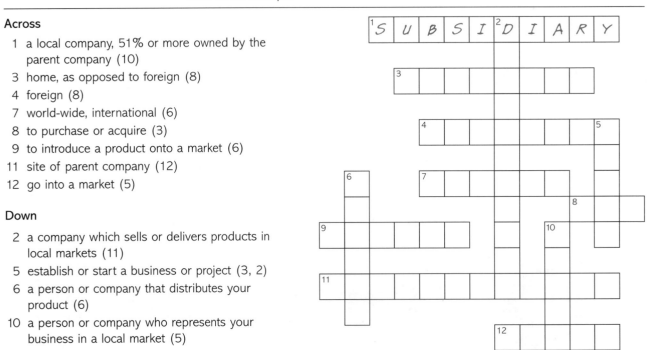

3 Complete these sentences with the prepositions.

into	up	for	out

1 We are looking .... an agent to represent us.
2 Setting .... a subsidiary might be the best option for us.
3 It's going to be difficult to break .... this new market.
4 The local community was very worried when we bought .... the main employer in the town.
5 I think we should be cautious about going .... this market.
6 Acquiring a company will speed .... our penetration of the market.
7 We are working .... a deal with a major distributor.
8 Could you look .... the phone numbers of agents in the Marseilles area?

4 learning tips

Notice how some verbs combine with different prepositions, e.g. the verb *to look* can combine with *for*, *at*, *after*, *up* or *into*. Use one of these combinations to complete each of the examples below.

a .... the picture. Isn't it beautiful?
b .... the telephone number. It's in the book.
c .... the reasons. We need to understand why the project failed.
d will you help me .... a flat? I need somewhere to live.
e .... the children, will you? We're going out.

Use your dictionary to identify key combinations for these verbs: *to come*, *to get*, *to make*, *to take*. Write an example sentence for each one.

reading

1 Read the article about doing business abroad. In most of the lines there is one extra word. It is either grammatically incorrect or does not fit in with the meaning of the text. If a line is correct, write CORRECT. If there is an extra word in the line, write it in CAPITAL LETTERS.

Doing business internationally

0	All of international business people need to be adaptable. They need to adapt to the	*OF*
00	different business cultures in their markets. A key area of behaviour is negotiation.	*CORRECT*
01	Strategies and tactics can vary enormously from a country to country. In the	....
02	United States, there is a very strong demand to get down to the business quickly, put your	....
03	cards on the table and not waste time if there is no prospect of a deal. With this	....
04	contrasts greatly with Japan where the rituals of this business negotiation,	....
05	especially at the start are given more for value. It is important to devote time to	....
06	building understanding through with your business partner. In this way both	....
07	parties can be make sure that conflict is avoided whatever the outcome of the	....
08	negotiation. In many US company cultures, conflict is being seen as a positive	....
09	force – by bringing issues of difference out into the open, they can be resolved and	....
10	people can move on more than quickly. In traditional Japanese business culture,	....
11	long-term business relationships based on mutual interests are at the middle heart of	....
12	doing business. American and Japanese business people need to adapt to the different pace	....

of doing business.

2 Read the article about dress codes. Choose the best sentence from below to fill each of the gaps. For each gap 1–5, mark one letter (A–G). Do not use any letter more than once.

dress codes

The dotcom boom at the end of last century had many effects on our behaviour at work. Industry observers have commented for years about the more relaxed style of the hi-tech start-up companies. Flat, non-hierarchical structures and a very informal communication style are two symptoms of this style which can be observed from within one of these companies. (0) ......*G*......

For years the dark suit, the plain white shirt and a sober choice of tie have been the corporate uniform of men at work. (1)................. Large organisations even had a written dress code which specified the limited range of colours and styles that the employee could choose from. Only in the so-called creative industries such as advertising were employees encouraged to show their individuality.

Towards the end of the twentieth century, we began to see the earliest signs that the days of corporate conformity were coming to an end. Some companies introduced casual Fridays on which employees could celebrate the approaching weekend by discarding their suits and ties and putting on chinos and sports shirts. (2).................

These developments move at different speeds in different parts of the world. The impetus, as with many business trends, comes from America, and it is here that you are most likely to see the above-mentioned jeans and T-shirt worn by the CEO of a Silicon Valley-based electronics multinational. (3)................. The feeling in these institutions is that they still need to adapt to the customers' cultures rather than impose their own.

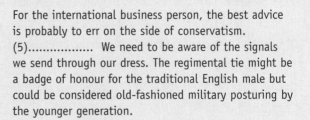

Business behaviour is not only influenced by the States. Climate and culture also have a large role to play. In many Asian cultures, business people dress conservatively but, if it's hot, they do not feel obliged to wear jackets. (4)................. The chic little black dress might be the ultimate in good dress sense to a French secretary but much too flimsy for a businessperson brought up in a Muslim community.

For the international business person, the best advice is probably to err on the side of conservatism. (5)................. We need to be aware of the signals we send through our dress. The regimental tie might be a badge of honour for the traditional English male but could be considered old-fashioned military posturing by the younger generation.

A However, in many cases jeans and T-shirts were not encouraged at that time.

B Looking too smart is definitely preferable to appearing too casual.

C Dress is a sign of the internal culture of the organisation.

D In contrast, European companies often make distinctions between staff who work face-to-face with customers as opposed to the back-office boys.

E Women joining these companies were expected to conform by wearing dark suits and conservative blouses.

F In addition, businesswomen in many countries continue to wear traditional dress and may be offended by Western women who they feel are dressed provocatively.

G The most visible external sign of this relaxed style is the way that most employees tend to dress down.

listening

1 🎧 You will hear five short recordings. For each recording, decide what the speaker's job is. Write one letter (A–H) next to the number of the recording. Do not use any letter more than once.

1 .... A Agent
2 .... B Embassy official
3 .... C Trade Fair Organiser
4 .... D Manager in acquired company
5 .... E Distributor
                    F Head of Subsidiary
                    G Export Manager
                    H Manager's Personal Assistant

2 🎧 You will hear another five recordings about working internationally. For each recording, decide what sort of challenge the speaker is talking about. Write one letter (A–H) next to the number of the recording. Do not use any letter more than once.

1 .... A Communication
2 .... B Cultural
3 .... C Personal
4 .... D Delivery
5 .... E Pricing
                    F Financial
                    G Paperwork
                    H Time management

language in use: conditionals 0, 1 and 2

Write full sentences using the conditional type given in brackets: zero conditional (0), first conditional (1), or second conditional (2).

Example
we export to Iran > we need an export licence (1)
If we export to Iran, we'll need an export licence.

1 we set up a local subsidiary > we hire local staff (2)
2 you visit the local embassy > you meet the commercial officer (1)
3 we acquire AFB > our sales double (2)
4 international business increase > there are more travel delays (1)
5 we develop our export markets > we need English language expertise (2)
6 there are public holidays abroad > the telephones much quieter (0)
7 we recruit a local branch manager > he / she have to speak English (1)
8 we not find an agent > we delay entry to the market (1)
9 we not get a permit > we have to cancel the transport (1)
10 I be you > I visit the subsidiary myself (2)

writing

1 James Richards recently visited Germany to look into extending his agency's networks there. Look at the extracts (1–11) from his report. Match the extracts with their function (a–d).

a Purpose
b Facts
c Comments (impressions)
d Recommendations

Market trip to Germany: Frankfurt

1 In the evening I attended a local Chamber of Commerce meeting.
2 We should draft an agency agreement for Frank Plotz to consider.
3 Frank Plotz seems to be the ideal candidate.
4 Both these meetings were disappointing.
5 The purpose of the trip was to extend our agency network in Germany.
6 I had organised two meetings in advance.
7 The first meeting was with Petra Kelly of Hartmann Import & Export.
8 We had a very fruitful discussion.
9 The second meeting was with Karl-Heinz Reutemann.
10 During the evening I was introduced to Frank Plotz, an independent agent.
11 I suggest we offer him our usual terms and conditions to act as an agent.

2 Put the extracts (1–11) in exercise 1 in the correct order to form his report.

fun and games

Match the flag with the correct country and then write in the languages.

country	flag	language
1 New Zealand		
2 United Kingdom		
3 Jamaica		
4 Japan		
5 Denmark		
6 Brazil	a	Portuguese
7 Saudi Arabia		
8 Wales		
9 Canada		
10 Greece		

a

b

c

d

e
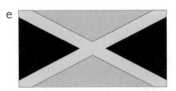

f

g

h

i

j

unit 10 sales

vocabulary

1 Match the sales literature (1–5) with the type of information it communicates (a–e).

1 company brochure   a name, title and contact details

2 business card   b product information including technical specifications

3 catalogue   c overview of company and products

4 leaflet   d additional or new product information

5 price list   e product or service prices

2 Rewrite the following sentences using the verb form of the underlined word and make any necessary changes.

Example
We organised underline{delivery} of the goods for 15 September.
We delivered the goods on 15 September.

1 The <u>negotiation</u> went on late into the night.
We ....

2 They sent an <u>invoice</u> before we received delivery.
They ....

3 We agreed a <u>discount</u> of nearly 15%.
The price ....

4 There was an <u>exhibition</u> of their products on the main stand.
They ....

5 There will be a <u>demonstration</u> of the new product later today.
We ....

6 Our customers showed a high level of <u>satisfaction</u> with our new model.
Our customers ....

7 We are going to send a <u>replacement</u> for the goods damaged in transit.
We ....

8 Good sales people need to learn how to give <u>priorities</u> to their calls.
Good ....

3 Complete the sentences with the words below.

close	delay	enquiry	form	leads	placed	prospects	stand

1 We booked a small .... measuring 2 m x 2 m in the main exhibition hall.

2 There are a lot of .... which we need to follow up on.

3 Have you dealt with that sales .... we received this morning?

4 We need to identify who are the best .... – in other words who has got the most sales potential.

5 Our main customer in Germany .... an order for 50,000 units.

6 Have you filled in the order ....? I need to send it off straight away.

7 We need to .... the sale before the end of the negotiation.

8 There was a ten-hour .... in delivery.

4 learning tips

Keep a note of new vocabulary. Writing down the words will help you to activate them. Always try to maximise the value of a new word, e.g. make sure you learn the opposites as well. Write the opposite of these words.

0 effective ...*ineffective*...   4 confident ....

1 efficient ....   5 patient ....

2 successful ....   6 polite ....

3 reliable ....   7 professional ....

reading

Look at the statements below and the information about training courses. Which course (A, B, C or D) does each statement 1–7 refer to? For each statement 1–7, mark one letter (A, B, C or D). You will need to use some of these letters more than once.

1 This is an active course where other people give you their opinions on your performance.
2 This course deals with translating what a customer wants into actual sales.
3 You will be introduced to a system for processing customer information.
4 It helps sales people finalise the deal.
5 You will learn how to overcome customer excuses.
6 You need to understand yourself as well as understand your customers.
7 You will analyse the personalities of other members of your sales team.

TRAINING COURSES

A Closing the sale

This course focuses on the final and absolutely vital phase of the sales process.

Do you have difficulty getting the customer to sign on the dotted line? Do your monthly sales figures disappoint you and your Sales Manager? If the answer is yes, this course is the one for you. We will be looking at the transition from establishing the need to making the sale.

B Rapport building

Selling is 80% about relationships. The keys to success are self-knowledge and customer knowledge. Starting with a 360-degree profile we will be building your understanding of your own strengths and weaknesses. Then we will be looking at the strengths and weaknesses of the rest of your team and focusing on the relationships. This will be the springboard to some real learning as we simulate the sales relationship. A really insightful course which will lead to greater understanding and skill.

C Customer management

A two day course which introduces you to a key resource – the CMT – the Customer Management Tool. Based on the very successful CDB – an easy-to-use customer database – the CMT is a powerful tool. It allows you to actively manage your customers and so maximise sales. Sales action planning becomes transparent and a really effective way to manage yourself and your team.

D Dealing with objections

An objection can kill the sale just at the moment you thought you had it all signed and sealed! The customer hasn't got the budget, the competitor has a long-standing relationship, the price is not flexible enough. Dealing with these sorts of objections is the real skill of selling. This one-day workshop is based on role-plays and feedback. Our workshop leader – Pat Niven – will take you through the key steps to dealing with objections and then give you the chance to put your new-found skill into practice.

listening

You will hear three telephone conversations, all concerning one order. Write one or two words or a number in the numbered spaces on the notes or e-mail below.

Conversation 1 (Questions 1–4)
Look at the notes below. You will hear a customer calling about an order.

Telephone message	KIEV SUPPLIES
For attention of	*Ludmilla*
Call from	(1)...........................
Subject	*Order for* (2)........................... *pipe brackets –* (3)........................... *batch not arrived yet.*
Action	*Call back immediately:* *tel no: 075686* (4)...........................

Conversation 2 (Questions 5–8)
Look at the notes below. You will hear the return call from the supplier.

INTERNATIONAL PIPELINES INC.

Telephone message

Call from Kiev Supplies (5)...........................

Subject Delivery of pipe brackets

Message Delivery made as planned to (6)........................... site (Kharkov).
Delivery note no: (7)........................... at (8)...........................
yesterday. Please call back.

Conversation 3 (Questions 9–12)
Look at the e-mail below. You will hear the customer calling the supplier again.

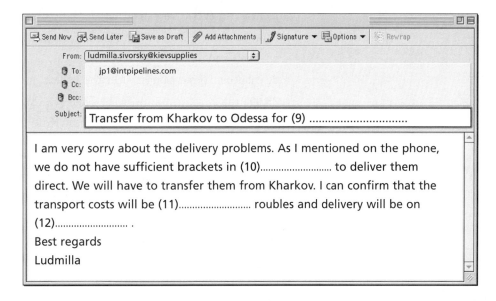

From: ludmilla.sivorsky@kievsupplies
To: jp1@intpipelines.com
Cc:
Bcc:
Subject: Transfer from Kharkov to Odessa for (9) ....

I am very sorry about the delivery problems. As I mentioned on the phone, we do not have sufficient brackets in (10)........................... to deliver them direct. We will have to transfer them from Kharkov. I can confirm that the transport costs will be (11)........................... roubles and delivery will be on (12)........................... .
Best regards
Ludmilla

language in use: the passive

1 Change the e-mail below so that the verbs underlined are in the passive rather than the active voice. The first one has been done for you.

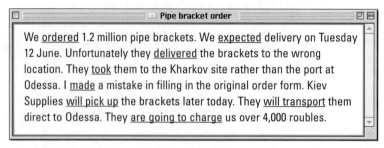

> **Pipe bracket order**
>
> We <u>ordered</u> 1.2 million pipe brackets. We <u>expected</u> delivery on Tuesday 12 June. Unfortunately they <u>delivered</u> the brackets to the wrong location. They <u>took</u> them to the Kharkov site rather than the port at Odessa. I <u>made</u> a mistake in filling in the original order form. Kiev Supplies <u>will pick up</u> the brackets later today. They <u>will transport</u> them direct to Odessa. They <u>are going to charge</u> us over 4,000 roubles.

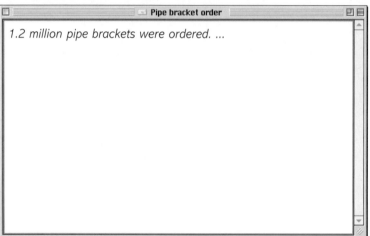

> **Pipe bracket order**
>
> *1.2 million pipe brackets were ordered. ...*

2 Complete the sales report with the verbs in the list below. You will need to use the passive and the active voice.

anticipate	increase	prepare	run	visit
distribute	launch (x2)	reach	show	withdraw

SALES REPORT

The ZX78 (1)........................ two years ago. During the first few months, an extensive marketing and sales campaign (2)........................ . TV ads (3)........................ on all the main channels and our sales force (4)........................ all the major distributors. Three months after the launch, monthly sales of 25,000 (5)........................ . The ZX78 (6)........................ through major retail outlets such as KEYMART and SAFCO.

In the second year, we (7)........................ a new version of the ZX – the ZX80. We (8)........................ sales by nearly 15%. The ZX78 (9)........................ from production at the end of last year and a third generation model (10)........................ for launch later this year. So far this year sales have reached their targets and we (11)........................ faster growth in the second half of the year.

writing

Geoff Masters is a Customer Services Assistant at Truscotts, an electrical components supplier. There have been problems with two of Truscotts deliveries. Use the information in the table below to complete the e-mails from Geoff to the two customers.

DELIVERY LOG

Customer	Ref No	Delivery address	Goods for delivery	Signature on delivery	Comment
H. Findale	200198	995 Londale	23 x VXE-222 connectors		Plant closed Left note
Terrys	200199	Mansion House	2 x TPH-16 lamps	Diana Long	1 x TPH-16 lamp damaged in transit Promised replacement next day

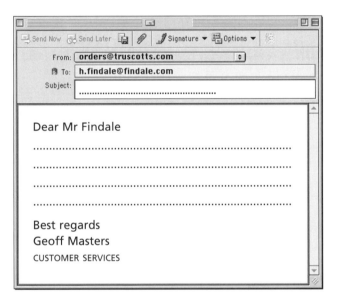

From: orders@truscotts.com
To: h.findale@findale.com
Subject: ....

Dear Mr Findale

....
....
....

....

Best regards
Geoff Masters
CUSTOMER SERVICES

From: orders@truscotts.com
To: dlong@terrys.com
Subject: ....

Dear Ms Long

....
....
....
....

Best regards
Geoff Masters
CUSTOMER SERVICES

fun and games

Match the type of salesperson (1–5) with the correct definition (a–e). Which type of salesperson do you prefer?

1 The order taker
2 The hard seller
3 The soft seller
4 The friend
5 The problem solver

a He / She is absolutely focused on the sale – pushing for closure.
b He / She is principally interested in building a relationship, tying the customer to the salesman and therefore the product.
c He / She shows concern and interest for the customer but also is informative about the product.
d He / She places the product before the customer and expects it to sell itself.
e He / She shows interest in the customer but not personally. He / She aims to meet the needs of the customer.

unit 11 motivation

vocabulary

1 Replace the underlined word in each sentence with a word or expression with the same meaning from the list below.

compensation	holiday	perks	objective
encouragement	performance reward	promotion opportunities	reduced hours

1 Our annual <u>leave</u> has to be taken during August when the factory closes down.
2 My <u>goal</u> is to earn enough to retire when I am 55.
3 The company is offering employees <u>an incentive</u> to take early retirement.
4 Once you reach 50, your <u>prospects</u> decrease considerably.
5 Since my promotion, my <u>pay</u> package includes a company car.
6 Most employees would prefer a bigger salary rather than more <u>fringe benefits</u>.
7 A thirteenth month salary is a type of <u>bonus</u> for high levels of productivity.
8 I would prefer <u>time off in lieu</u> the following week rather than overtime pay.

2 Which words a–j can be combined with the three key words 1–3 below? (Some can be combined with more than one key word.)

1 leave 　　 2 pay 　　 3 working

a conditions 　 c basic 　 e sick 　 g hours 　 i unpaid
b maternity 　 d day 　 f annual 　 h package 　 j full

3 Use some of the combinations from exercise 2 to complete the sentences.

1 In most countries, mothers take several months' .... before and after their children are born. In some countries, they receive .... while they are off work, in others it is reduced.

2 It was the money and the holiday that really attracted me to this job. I suppose I took it for the .... and the generous ....

3 In some countries, after two days off ill, you must send a doctor's note so that you can receive ....

4 I've used up all my holiday so I am trying to persuade my boss to allow me some ....

5 The .... are very long and the .... before overtime is not very good.

6 Our .... is nine to five and the .... are good.

4 learning tips

To actively learn a new word, you need to put it into an example which is memorable for you.

Examples

perk
'The best perk of my job is free flights.'

incentive
'If the tax rates are too high, there's no incentive to earn more.'

Think of a memorable sentence for each of these words:
leave, *promotion*, *compensation*.

listening

1 🎧 You will hear five short recordings. For each recording, decide the reason for job satisfaction. Write one letter (A–H) next to the number of the recording. Do not use any letter more than once.

1	A salary
2	B working hours
3	C promotion opportunities
4	D perks
5	E office facilities
	F job security
	G holidays
	H staff relations

2 🎧 You will hear another five recordings. For each recording, decide what sort of financial incentive the speaker is talking about. Write one letter (A–H) next to the number of the recording. Do not use any letter more than once.

1	A Christmas bonus
2	B share options
3	C profit share
4	D company car
5	E train season ticket
	F sales commission
	G overtime payments
	H pension scheme

Read the article about work preferences and the questions below. For each question 1–6, mark one letter (A, B, C or D) for the answer you choose.

Profiling our behaviour at work

Motivation comes from doing a job well and most of us work best when we are doing something we like. To improve our own motivation and performance, it can help to better understand the types of work we have to do and our own individual preferences – in other words, how we like to behave at work. Charles Margerison and Dick McCann, two management psychologists, have developed Team Management Systems as a powerful tool for understanding individual and team preferences. The work preference model is based on four key dimensions.

1 Establishing relationships

This measures how you like to interact with people at work – at one extreme, very extrovert behaviour is seen in those that like to socialise, network, take on a great variety of tasks and rarely settle on one thing for long. On the other hand, introverts feel much less need to mix, tend to focus on the job in hand and don't like to be interrupted.

2 Information handling

This contrasts the practical person who tends to focus very much on the present, gets on with the job and is very task-focused, with people with a creative leaning who seem to have their heads in the clouds. Creative types are not so good at routine, tend to be more future-oriented and need variety to challenge them.

3 Decision making

Analytical types make their decisions based on objective evidence, have a strong sense of rules and procedures and can be seen as a little cold-hearted. Those of us who are influenced more by our beliefs tend to use subjective criteria when making decisions. These types have a strong sense of right and wrong and are often very committed to their point of view.

4 Organisation

This dimension contrasts structured types who are usually very time conscious, concentrate on concluding the task, and are less interested in time-consuming debate, with those of a more flexible nature. Flexible types are more disorganised, more open to change if the date changes and not so good at deadlines.

These four dimensions are used to profile individual preferences so that you can think about your own style of work. Once you have a better understanding of your own motivation, you can then start to look at the profiles of other members of your team.

1 Higher motivation and better performance can come from
   A doing a job well.
   B understanding our own preferences.
   C doing different types of work.
   D understanding each other.

2 Extroverts like to
   A focus on a few tasks.
   B settle on a single task.
   C have several different things to do.
   D concentrate on the job at hand.

3 The information dimension contrasts
   A present with future orientation.
   B boring with interesting people.
   C innovation with creativity.
   D time-conscious people with less punctual types.

4 Analytical types are
   A committed to a definite point of view.
   B guided by a clear set of principles.
   C often inflexible.
   D inclined to respect rules.

5 Flexible types are
   A good at finishing tasks.
   B time conscious.
   C resistant to change.
   D not so time conscious.

6 Once you have profiled your own preferences, the next step is to
   A criticise your colleagues.
   B understand your colleagues' preferences.
   C profile your competitors.
   D profile the type of work you should do.

language in use: the *-ing* form

Complete the sentences with the following verbs in the *-ing* form.

be	cover	get	reduce	sit	talk
complain	do	motivate	save	take	travel

1 We are all looking forward to .... our Christmas bonus.

2 .... the workforce is the most important factor in successful management.

3 Don't you just feel like .... the day off?

4 Would you mind .... for me at work? I have to go to a funeral.

5 He's a good boss because he tells you what you're good at and bad at ....

6 .... an air steward suits me as I enjoy ....

7 There's no point .... They are not going to change their minds.

8 The company are considering .... our salaries by 5% in order to get through this tough period.

9 I have been .... money towards my pension since I started work.

10 She's always working on something new – she hates just .... and .... all day long.

writing

You are an HR Manager. You are responsible for introducing an incentive scheme to motivate the workforce. Before the programme starts, you want to get some reactions to your ideas from the rest of the management team.
Complete the memo below:

- mentioning the three options – Christmas bonus, performance bonus, profits share.
- asking for their opinions.
- giving a deadline for their feedback.

The memo should be 40–50 words in total.

memo

to	Management staff
from	Joe Wild, HR Manager
date	2 June
subject	Incentive Scheme

As you all know, we ....
There are ....
1 Christmas bonus
2 Performance bonus
3 Profits share
I would be interested to know ....
Please .... by 15 June.

fun and games

Match each motivation 1–3 with the appropriate incentives a–g.

1 I am motivated by the place. I need to feel it's a fun place to be.
2 I think most people are motivated by one thing – and we all know what that is!
3 Motivation comes from inside. You've got to feel your work is worth doing.

Incentives
a Extra holidays
b Productivity bonus
c Company excursion to Disneyland
d Extra responsibilities
e Change in office environment
f Company car
g New code of ethics

unit 12 customer service

vocabulary

1 Complete the flow chart with the following words.

build	negotiate	provide	renew	request	win

1 .... a deal

2 .... a new customer

3 .... top-quality service

4 .... customer feedback

5 .... customer loyalty

6 .... contract

2 Match the expressions 1–6 with their explanations a–f.

1 acknowledge a customer   a win a customer over to doing business with you
2 hold on to a customer   b keep a customer
3 woo a customer   c build up a long-term relationship with a customer
4 lose a customer   d show a customer that you know they are there
5 approach a customer   e make contact with a customer
6 develop a customer   f fail to keep a customer

3 learning tips

One way to remember new vocabulary is to tell or create stories which use the new words.

Example   assistant – exchange – voucher – returns policy – Head Office

I took back a shirt on Saturday. I told the assistant that it didn't fit. He said I could exchange it for another shirt or take a voucher to the same value; that was the company's returns policy. When I said I would write to the Head Office, he just gave me the address!

Make up your own story which links these words together. You may use them in any order.
customer – shop – return – refund – disgruntled – complain – Head Office – letter – customer satisfaction

reading

1 Read the article below about call centres. In most of the lines there is an extra word. It is either grammatically incorrect or does not fit with the meaning of the text. If a line is correct, write CORRECT. If there is an extra word in the line, write it in CAPITAL LETTERS.

Call centres in crisis

0	Customer satisfaction levels are falling in Europe and Australia, while in America	*CORRECT*
00	according to recent reports levels have been declined for a second straight quarter. The	*BEEN*
01	American Customer Satisfaction Index (ACSI) has fell by 0.6% for the first quarter	....
02	of this year, now standing in at 72.2 out of a possible 100. The five sectors studied	....
03	in the first quarter of the year were for utilities, parcel delivery/express mail,	....
04	airlines, telecommunications and hotels. The ongoing cost-cutting exercise which is	....
05	hurting service delivery and, despite IT investments in call centres to the fine	....
06	tune of over $20 billion yearly, very few companies are getting the needed Return On	....
07	Investment. Many TV commercials broadcast today are by saying 'call us now,	....
08	you won't be put on hold in a call centre.' Perhaps because the call centre industry	....
09	is an easy target for customer dissatisfaction, it seems is becoming more frequently	....
10	associated with bad or indifferent service. At the same time, the move as by major	....
11	corporations to set up call-handling centres in low-cost locations such as India	....
12	is not for helping this situation, nor is it improving the perception of the industry	....
	as a whole.	

2 Read the article about customer service over the phone. Choose the best word to fill each gap from A, B, C or D below. For each question 1–15, mark one letter (A, B, C or D).

Dealing with customers over the phone

First impressions are (0).......*B*...... over the phone. Prospective customers are considering (1)................. or not to do business with you. Irate customers are (2)................. how helpful and competent you are. For best results, incorporate two easy elements: pleasantness and sincerity.

Pleasantness: A pleasant greeting is (3)................. to a successful call because it sets the stage emotionally. In general, listeners tend to (4)................. or 'catch' the emotional states of speakers. In other words, people (5)................. to what they hear. If we answer the phone gruffly, chances are the caller will become gruff. If we answer the phone pleasantly, chances are the caller will be pleasant, and we all know which caller is easier to work with.

One of the easiest ways to (6)................. an emotional state quickly is to concentrate carefully on your (7)................. language. I recommend that professionals establish a (8)................. before answering the phone. In order to sound pleasant, we need to be carrying ourselves accordingly. My routine is to sit up on the (9)................. of my seat, pull my shoulders back, take a deep (10)................., smile, let the phone ring twice, then answer. I never answer my phone unless I've gone through this process. My business is too (11)................. . Sometimes I'll even stand before I answer the phone if I need an extra jolt of (12)................. .

Sincerity: I am against scripting greetings because they sound insincere and (13)................. to irritate callers, and discourage employees. Scripted greetings usually include some kind of (14)................. . 'Hello. It's a beautiful day here at the XYZ Company.' Now I don't care where you work. It can't be that good all day. You want the greeting to be (15)................., which also makes it easier to sound pleasant consistently.

0	A useful	B critical	C effective	D interesting
1	A how	B why	C whether	D if
2	A deciding	B thinking	C concluding	D agreeing
3	A needed	B essential	C urgent	D necessary
4	A act	B mime	C pretend	D mirror
5	A respond	B talk	C speak	D answer
6	A evolve	B have	C attain	D be
7	A foreign	B body	C new	D child
8	A style	B ritual	C behaviour	D rule
9	A point	B corner	C kerb	D edge
10	A puff	B sigh	C breath	D pull
11	A worthwhile	B important	C interesting	D enjoyable
12	A energy	B life	C fear	D electricity
13	A mean	B tend	C try	D aim
14	A saying	B motto	C slogan	D quote
15	A open	B natural	C straight	D clear

listening

🎧 You will hear three telephone conversations or messages. Write one or two words or a number in the numbered spaces on the notes or forms below.

Conversation 1 (Questions 1–4)

Look at the notes below. You will hear a message about travel arrangements.

answerphone message	5-STAR TRAVEL

Date	14 June Time 18.45
Caller	Sally (1).............................
Message	Tickets not arrived. Flight departure on (2)............................
Booking ref	(3).............................
Action	Call back to arrange pick-up Tel: 09467 (4).............................

Conversation 2 (Questions 5–8)

Look at the form below. You will hear a man calling about a delay.

ATC PARKING LOG

Customer	Car Type	Flight No
Josh Stanton	Laguna..........	(5).......................
Arr Time	**Car Registration**	**Pick-up point**
(6).......................	(7).......................	(8).......................

Conversation 3 (Questions 9–12)

Look at the form below. You will hear a woman complaining about a lost suitcase.

AIRCARE BAGGAGE HANDLING	REPORT FORM

Passenger Name: (9)........................ Donovan   Action: Deliver to Mercury Hotel
Arrival Date: (10)............................   (note: check with Mermaid)
Flight No: GB987   Call back Jenny on
Luggage Tag No: GB987 (11)............................   0278 (12)............................

language in use: third conditional and past modals

1 Make conditional sentences by combining the two parts. Follow the example.

Example
save more money for the trip > travel first class
If we had saved more money for the trip, we would have travelled first class.

1 travel first class > not meet an old friend in economy
2 not meet an old friend in economy > sleep on the flight
3 sleep on the flight > not feel so tired when we land
4 not feel so tired when we land > get to the car rental more quickly
5 get to the car rental more quickly > not miss the last available car
6 not miss the last available car > not catch the bus into town

2 Talk to a partner about recent trips they have made. Ask them how they would have reacted in these situations: lost passport; missed connection; lost luggage.

writing

You work in the Customer Service department of a Travel Agent's. You have collated the customer satisfaction response forms for June and made some notes. You have also drafted the monthly report below for your Head Office. Read the information carefully. Then read the report and correct any mistakes in the grammar or content. There are eight mistakes.

Collated results of customer satisfaction response forms

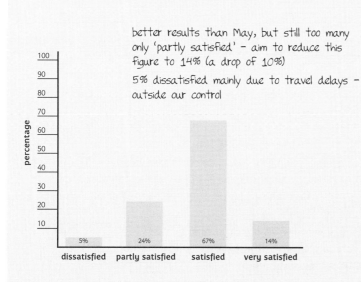

better results than May, but still too many only 'partly satisfied' – aim to reduce this figure to 14% (a drop of 10%)

5% dissatisfied mainly due to travel delays – outside our control

Main areas of complaint	No. of complaints
Delays	35
Hotel standard	22
Lost luggage	26
Others	15

- delays caused by air traffic control. If not, level around 20
- hotel standard: Hotel Mercury 18 complaints – problems with drains

MONTHLY REPORT
Subject: Satisfaction levels
Month: June

During June, the results were more better than in May. However, there were still too much customers (24%) who were only partly satisfied. Our aim is to reduce this figure to 10% by the end of the year.

The 5% figure for dissatisfied customers were mainly due to travel delays what unfortunately were outside our control.

The major cause of complaint were delays. However, if there were not air traffic control problems the level would have been 20. 22 of the hotel complaints were about the Hotel Mercury where they had problems with drains.

fun and games

What have these customers bought and what sort of compensation might they expect?

1 I know I asked for it rare, but I still expected you to cook it a bit!

2 In the brochure there was a swimming pool with a bar. When we got there, all we found was a hole in the ground.

3 I can't believe it. They're two sizes too big and you measured me in the shop.

4 When I tried to release the handbrake, the lever just came off in my hand.

5 The motor packed in on the 366th day. We must have lost $300 worth of frozen food.

unit 13 business ethics

vocabulary

1 Complete the sentences about different stakeholders with the words below.

banks	community	customers	employees	share holders	suppliers

1 The .... of a company have a big stake in its future. Without a prosperous future, they have no jobs.

2 .... are vital for their contribution to the final quality of the product and also in meeting the demands of production.

3 The local .... is usually a very important stakeholder. The prosperity of the region as a whole is tied up with the success of the company.

4 .... need or want the company to continue producing the service or product so that they can buy it.

5 Publicly quoted companies have to consider their .... Their nvestment in the company ensures the necessary financial support. The profitability guarantees their dividends.

6 Many companies need to have very close relationships with their .... Their long-term financial stability usually depends on this relationship.

2 Complete the sentences with the words and phrases below.

bribe	ethical	low labour cost	support	values
code of ethics	legislation	redundancies	toxic	

1 Relocation of the company's main production unit to a .... region will inevitably lead to ....

2 The line between a .... and a gift is very difficult to draw. In some cultures, it is customary to give some kind of present when meeting a potential customer.

3 Many companies have drawn up a .... which aims to enshrine the .... and morals of the organisation.

4 Some companies have become actively involved in their local community. This may not just mean providing financial ...., but also giving employees time off to work on local projects.

5 .... investment funds have been set up to attract investors wanting to see their money used in businesses which are sensitive to both local and global issues.

6 Environmental .... has been considerably toughened recently. Companies have been forced to think twice before discharging their .... waste into the local river.

3 Rewrite the following sentences. Use the word in brackets rather than the word underlined and make any necessary changes.

Example

A code of ethics can simply <u>enhance</u> your image. (enhancement)
A code of ethics can simply be used for enhancement of your image.

1 They have made a lot of employees <u>redundant</u>. (redundancies)
   There have been ....

2 The employees don't show any real <u>commitment</u> to their jobs. (committed)
   The employees are not ....

3 Employees sometimes do <u>voluntary</u> work in the local community. (volunteer)
   Employees ....

4 The company has sent staff on <u>secondments</u> to India. (seconded)
   The company ....

5 There has been a lot of <u>bribery</u> by the business community to get what it wants.
   (bribed)
   The business community has ....

6 This brand of trainers was popular until the <u>discovery</u> that they were made in
   sweatshops. (discovered)
   This brand of trainers was popular until it was ....

7 Nowadays, job candidates are taking more <u>interest</u> in a prospective company's
   code of ethics. (interested)
   Nowadays, job candidates are more ....

8 <u>Pollution</u> in the River Trask from the Arcon factory has reduced considerably over
   the last few years. (polluted)
   Arcon has ....

4 learning tips

Remember that some verbs are used with certain prepositions. Make sure you learn the verb plus preposition. Match these verbs (1–8) with the correct preposition. In some cases, there is more than one preposition.

about	for	of	on	to	up

1 to draw   5 to be aware

2 to opt   6 to depend

3 to think   7 to admit

4 to care   8 to look forward

Write an example sentence for each combination.

Look at the statements below and the texts about four key principles of the Fair Trade Federation. Which text (A, B, C or D) does each statement 1–7 refer to? For each statement 1–7, mark one letter (A, B, C or D). You will need to use some of these letters more than once.

Example

0 This principle allows producers to pay for the essentials of life.   *A*

1 This principle encourages customers to buy goods which have been produced ethically.
2 This principle discourages the use of profit for the short-term gain of outsiders.
3 This principle is aimed at returning the maximum margin to the producer.
4 This principle encourages the long-term protection of the landscape.
5 This principle encourages workers to join together.
6 This principle allows producers to deal directly with their markets.
7 This principle encourages sensitivity to local customs and way of life.

Fair Trade Federation: four key principles

A Fair pay

Producers are paid fairly for their products, which means that workers are paid at least that country's minimum wage. Since the minimum wage is often not enough for basic survival, whenever feasible, workers are paid a living wage, which enables them to cover basic needs, including food, shelter, education and health care for their families. Paying fair wages does not necessarily mean that products cost the consumer more. Since Fair Trade Organisations bypass exploitative middlemen and work directly with producers, they are able to cut costs and return a greater percentage of the retail price to the producers.

B Co-operation

Co-operatives and producer associations provide a healthy alternative to large-scale manufacturing and sweatshop conditions. Unprotected workers often earn below the minimum wage and most of the profits flow to foreign investors and local elites who have little interest in ensuring the long term health of the communities in which they work. By banding together, workers are able to access credit, reduce raw material costs and establish higher and more just prices for their products.

C Education

Fair Trade Organisations educate consumers about the importance of purchasing fairly traded products which support living wages and healthy working conditions. By providing information about producers' history, culture and living conditions, Fair Trade Organisations enhance cross-cultural understanding and respect between consumers and communities in the developing world.

D The environment

Fair Trade Organisations encourage producers to engage in environmentally friendly practices which manage and use local resources sustainably. Many FTO members work directly with producers in regions of high biodiversity to develop products based on sustainable use of their natural resources, giving communities an incentive to preserve their natural environments for future generations.

listening

🎧 You will hear an interview with Rosanne Field, Head of Corporate Affairs at Zintec, an international pharmaceutical company. She is being interviewed for a radio programme about ethics in business. For each question 1–8, mark one letter (A, B or C) for the correct answer.

1 The target for the corporate message is
   A all those with money in the company.
   B all those with a stake in the company.
   C all those with shares in the company.

2 The mission of Zintec is to
   A involve employees in the work of the company.
   B get financial support from shareholders.
   C produce remedies to improve the world's health.

3 The company's main target audience is
   A the doctors.
   B the patients.
   C the pharmacies.

4 The patients are important because
   A they test new drugs.
   B the treatments are for them.
   C they are well-informed.

5 The doctors' main concern is to
   A make their patients better.
   B be well-informed.
   C make medical breakthroughs.

6 Many medical associations have
   A banned doctors from accepting hospitality.
   B given doctors a strict code to follow.
   C allowed a mix of education and entertainment.

7 The pharmaceutical industry has a poor reputation because they have been
   A reintroducing drugs which were already available.
   B launching too many new drugs.
   C developing dangerous active substances.

8 Zintec has built a good name in the business through
   A fighting hard.
   B medical breakthroughs.
   C developing new and innovative treatments.

language in use: articles

Some of the following sentences contain mistakes. If a sentence is incorrect, make the necessary corrections by adding or deleting articles *a* or *the*.

1 The customer service is vital for all the organisations.
2 We have targeted youth of today as a most profitable market
3 We have introduced the code of ethics. This outlines underlying values which all the employees must subscribe to.
4 Our strategy in Third World has been approved by World Health Organisation.
5 We can accept gifts up to the value of $20.
6 In United Kingdom we give the tips to taxi drivers and hairdressers.
7 The line between the tip and the bribe is sometimes difficult to draw.
8 In the developing country, the petty corruption is probably more visible than in a developed country.
9 Large-scale corruption influences many aspects of the life in this country.
10 A behaviour is different in the country. There is much less corruption than in the town.

writing

Read the following report about ethical issues in the pharmaceutical industry and check for grammatical errors. (Notice the use of articles, tenses and verb agreements.) Correct the text and then rewrite it using appropriate section headings. Write 120–140 words.

> There are many issues which currently concern our industry. The first one is the issue of providing solutions for a developing world. Critics says that our industry does not invest enough in research to help the Third World. The second issue is the cost of new drugs. We are often accused of not making our products available at the reasonable prices. The third major issue is our relationship with the medical profession. Some people believes the relationship is too close and that we have too much influence over doctors. We need to show our critics that we invested heavily in new treatments for major diseases. We need to explain the cost of research and development. We also need to show the world that we support the medical profession but do not have power over it.

fun and games

Which of the following do you consider an ethical issue?

1 Creative accounting ('cooking the books') which gives a company's balance sheet a more positive look.
2 Enquiring about family status of female candidates before offering them a job.
3 Transferring production from high labour-cost regions to low labour-cost areas.
4 Cutting environmental budgets in order to protect jobs.
5 Giving jobs to family members.

unit 14 new directions

vocabulary

1 Match the traditional way of working (1–9) with the new practice (a–i) which has in some cases replaced it.

Traditional
1 closed door offices
2 daily travel to work
3 fixed desk
4 letters
5 multi-layered hierarchy
6 face-to-face meetings
7 typewriter
8 fixed line
9 limited job responsibilities

New
a flat organisation
b hot-desking
c video-conferencing
d desktop computer
e mobile telephone
f multi-tasking
g open-plan offices
h e-mails
i telecommuting

2 Complete the sentences using words or phrases from exercise 1.

1 My company has offices all over the world, so we often use .... when several people from different offices need to discuss something.

2 The biggest drawback with a .... is that the phone companies charge much more than they do for using a ....

3 What I really like about .... is the way you can communicate so easily with people around you.

4 I know of a novelist who still uses a .... for all her books – she says the noise of the keys helps her to think.

5 It was the .... that I found most difficult – I can't imagine how much time I spent stuck in traffic jams.

6 .... is being used with considerable success in companies where many of the staff spend much of their time away from the office.

7 For me there's no substitute for ...., where you can talk to a real person and not a phone line or a video screen.

8 Even in the modern technological age, ... are still an important way of communicating confidential information.

9 The great thing about .... is the speed at which you can get your message across to somebody – provided they have their computer switched on!

10 .... can sometimes create a feeling of isolation, but working from home rather than travelling to work frees up time to spend with family and friends.

3 Complete the table.

noun	adjective	opposite adjective
space	spacious	cramped
efficiency		
productivity		
co-operation		
accessibility		
flexibility		
stress		
professionalism		
availability		
noise		
expense		

4 Use a word from the table in exercise 2 to complete the sentences. In some cases, more than one word is possible.

1 He has moved to a remote island – one of the most .... places I can think of.

2 Spending three hours a day commuting to work is very ....

3 One of the arguments for the traditional workplace is that it encourages .... between colleagues.

4 A big problem with working from home is that you are .... 24 hours a day – colleagues can reach you at any time.

5 Subsidising season tickets for commuters is a very .... option.

6 We can all have .... days at work. The difference is that if you work from home, you can do something else .... like the washing or the cooking!

7 Most people believe that reducing the .... in our lives is a good thing, but some people maintain that .... work keeps you on your toes!

8 Working from home is much more .... for me. It allows me to plan my day as it suits me and in the end this makes me more ....

9 One of the problems with the open-plan office at work is that it's very .... – you can hardly hear yourself think.

10 Working from home can make you .... – not bothering to get dressed in the morning can mean you get sloppy in your work.

5 learning tips

It is very useful to be able to distinguish between the following types of words:

1 words that you personally need to be able to use when you speak and write
2 words you need to be able to understand when you read and listen
3 words that you are unlikely to need to use or understand.

Check the meanings of the following words in a good dictionary. Then classify them as type 1, 2 or 3. Write an example sentence for each of the type 1 words.

alter	cramped	flat	hierarchy	multilateral	remote
carry out	distant	folder	isolated	notion	video-conferencing
commute	enable	guru	keystroke	open-plan	virtual workstation

Read the article below about technology and changes at work. Choose the best sentence from below to fill each of the gaps. For each gap 1–5, mark one letter (A–G). Do not use any letter more than once.

When an American company recently took over a well-established French utilities concern they found that their styles of communicating greatly differed. The French company were using e-mail for their internal and external communication but continuing to follow the established channels. The Americans used e-mail in a far less structured way – they would e-mail their boss, their subordinates and their colleagues with the same information or idea. (0)..........*G*...... For many managers information can no longer be used as a tool of power – managing on a 'right to know' basis. The Internet and company intranets are breaking down both technological and social barriers.

Breaking down barriers

Technology is also eroding many other business practices. (1)................... The traditional way of communicating is best seen in the classic business letter with its polite and ritualistic language. E-mail is no respecter of these conventions: its inherent characteristics – immediacy and speed – do not encourage reflection and time given to the formulation of courteous replies. It encourages direct and often blunt communication which pays no attention to the traditional processes of relationship building.

The downside of all this speed of communication, however, is that there is no longer time to build trust. As face-to-face meetings are replaced by video-conferences and the leisurely lunch becomes a thing of the past, it raises the question of when we are going to get to know our business partners. (2)................... The orders are flowing in and the deliveries are going out on time. The turnover is rising and the profits doubling. But what about when the business hits a bad patch? This is when you need your suppliers to be understanding and your customers to look favourably at you, rather than the competition.

Technology brings many advantages for the worker but it also leads to a lot of stress. (3)................... Often only the leading directors have the luxury of their own PA. Everybody else has to handle their own correspondence, plan their business trips and manage their diaries. This usually has to be fitted in around all their main responsibilities such as market research and production planning. Because of this, managers have to work longer and longer hours to deal with all these tasks – both the little administrative ones and the vital strategic ones. (4)...................

Technology should free up time and we can certainly point to improvements. Finding information is now very much faster. Good databases and Internet search engines mean that we can quickly find that name, number or vital statistic. (5)................... Twenty years ago, people had to remember many more telephone numbers than they need to today, where we can now access this sort of information with menus and pre-set codes. Hopefully this frees us up to think about more important things.

A It is important that change is for the better.
B For example, traditionally formality and distance in business relationships have been maintained through the formal use of language.
C Easy access to information also means fewer demands on our memory.
D Maybe this does not matter so much when things are going well.
E It is not surprising, therefore, that employees often start to lose sight of the big picture and get bogged down in procedures.
F Many companies have cut back on secretarial support.
G This difference in behaviour meant a big adaptation for the local managers who had previously respected a power structure which was partly based on withholding information.

listening

1 🎧 You will hear five short recordings. For each recording, decide what sort of change in his/her working life the speaker has faced. Write one letter (A–H) next to the number of the recording. Do not use any letter more than once.

1 ....   A hot-desking
2 ....   B video-conferencing
3 ....   C management style
4 ....   D open-plan office
5 ....   E too much information
                       F telecommuting
                       G virtual training
                       H multi-tasking

2 🎧 You will hear another five recordings. For each recording, decide what the speaker predicts about the future of work. Write one letter (A–H) next to the number of the recording. Do not use any letter more than once.

1 ....   A expansion into space
2 ....   B virtual projects
3 ....   C later retirement
4 ....   D more free time
5 ....   E faster communication
                       F micro computers
                       G greater job mobility
                       H relocation to the country

language in use: degrees of future certainty

1 Complete the probability table with the modal verbs below. In some cases, more than one verb can be used.

could	may	might	should	will	won't

		impersonal	personal	modal use
100%	certain	It is certain/definite	I am sure	It (1)..................... happen
	probable	It is likely/probable	I expect	It (2)..................... happen
	possible	It is possible	I think	It (3)..................... happen
	improbable	It is unlikely	I doubt	It probably (4)..................... happen
0%	impossible	It is impossible	I am sure + neg	It (5)..................... happen

2 Complete the sentences with the expressions in the table in exercise 1.

1 There's a good chance he'll get early retirement. I .... he'll be gone by next month.
2 There's no chance of getting transferred. It just .... happen.
3 There's not much chance of this working. I .... it'll work.
4 It's certain that the technology will change. It .... change very soon.
5 There's a chance of getting through later today or you .... get him on his mobile number.
6 He .... get here by five, but it's unlikely.
7 There's no way we'll be ready on time. I .... we .... make it.
8 The trials are nearly finished so the system .... come on-line next year.

3 Talk to a partner about their future. Discuss the probability of the following happening: a change of job; a move to a new country; summers getting colder; buying a new car.

writing

Use the headings and expressions below to complete the report about the use of e-mail at work.

According to the survey	Findings	The purpose of this report
Another concern	Recommendations	This trend is likely to continue
Conclusions	The current situation	We recommend
E-mail use		

Subject: (1).......................................

(2)..................................... is to comment on current e-mail use and make recommendations for future changes.

(3).....................................
(4)....................................., e-mail usage has increased by 35% over the last year. (5)...................................... is that 55% of all e-mails are internal and the remaining external. Most of the increase has been in internal e-mails. (6)...................................... unless action is taken.

(7).....................................
We are using e-mail too much for internal communication. As a result, face-to-face communication has decreased. (8)..................................... is that personal contact is also decreasing with customers.

(9).....................................
(10)...................................... that employees do not send e-mails to colleagues working in nearby offices. We also feel that a morning and afternoon coffee breaks should be encouraged in order to give employees an opportunity to meet face to face.

fun and games

Look at sentences 1–6 below. Then decide what chance there is of these things happening in the next 50 years.

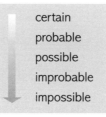

certain
probable
possible
improbable
impossible

1 Electric vehicles will be the principal form of transport.
2 China will become the dominant world economy.
3 Water will be the main source of power for industry.
4 You will need to be genetically tested before being hired for a new job.
5 Women will hold the majority of senior management positions.
6 E-commerce will gradually replace traditional retailing.

sample writing tasks

Writing Part 1   The following exercises will help to familiarise you with the requirements of the Writing test.

1   Read the exam task below and the sample answer.

     1   Can you find four grammatical mistakes?

     2   What mistake has the writer made when reading the question?

You are in charge of internal communications in a chemical company. You have recently carried out a survey of how e-mail is used internally. You need to tell the staff the conclusions of this survey and recommend appropriate action.

Write a memo to all staff:
- telling them that 65% of current e-mails are unnecessary.
- suggesting other ways of communicating.
- asking them to be more careful in their use of e-mails.

Write 40–50 words.

Sample memo

MEMO

TO   All staff

FROM   David Hoffman

SUBJECT   <u>Internal use of e-mail</u>

As a result of a survey recently carried out, the company discovered that 65% of e-mails are unnecessary and not related with the business.

The company reminds you to use other way of communicating for external issues, and suggest you more careful in the use of e-mail.

Thanks.

2   Read the exam task below and the sample answer on page 75.

     1   Can you find three grammatical mistakes?

     2   How could you improve the greeting and farewell?

You are in charge of an international project. You need to contact all the project team, reminding them about the next meeting.

Write an e-mail to the team:
- informing them of the date and location.
- asking them to confirm their arrival and departure times.
- requesting them to send project reports before the meeting.

Write 40–50 words.

Sample e-mail

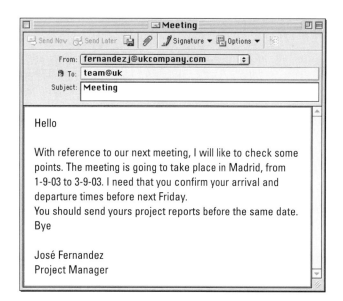

3 Read the exam task below and the two sample answers. Which is the better answer? Why?

> You are working late to prepare for an important meeting so will be late into work the next day. You need your assistant to carry out some tasks the following morning before you arrive.
>
> Write a note to your assistant:
> • telling her about the meeting.
> • asking her to call one of your customers to tell him the next delivery date.
> • reminding her to request provisional quantities for his next order.
>
> Write 40–50 words.

Sample note 1

I am delayed because I have been working very late last night. I need you to help me with these tasks:
– Call Mr. Kendall telling him that his delivery will arrive next Friday.
– Ask to our supplier to send us another lot of the AXB item for the next order.

Sample note 2

Maria,
I have been working late to prepare for this afternoon meeting so I will be late in the morning. Could you call Mr Anderson and inform the next delivery will be made on Friday? Please, don't forget to check provisional quantities for the order we have to deliver next week.

Thanks
R.B.

Writing Part 2

1 Read the exam task below and the Examiner's marking scheme.

> You work for a wine merchant. You have been asked to write a reply to a customer complaint. Look at the letter on which you have already made some notes. Then using all your notes, write your letter.
>
> Write 120–140 words.

10 Neverwindings
Salisbury
Wiltshire

14 June

Apologise for the late delivery, due to enormous demand

Apologise and express surprise

Dear Sirs

I recently responded to the special offer advertised in the national press. I filled in the order form six weeks ago and paid by credit card. The case of wine finally arrived yesterday and I celebrated by opening the first bottle. It was a major disappointment as it tasted sour.

I certainly do not want to risk opening any further bottles and would like you to reimburse me for the full cost.

Yours faithfully

Paul Gifford

Enclose a voucher for the full value of the order

Enclose latest catalogue – hope to receive new order

Examiner's marking scheme

Content	Should include all four of the notes from the customer's letter.
Organisation	The reason for writing should be made clear at the beginning of the letter. Paragraphs and linking devices should be used to present the content clearly and logically.
Format	In the form of a business letter, with a suitable opening and closing.
Register	The register should be formal and polite.
Target reader	The customer should understand the reason for the delay, appreciate the apology, understand the refund and feel encouraged to make a new order.

Now read the sample answer. Has the writer answered the question successfully?

Sample letter

18 June

Dear Mr Gifford

We are writing in connection with your letter of June 14. We are extremely sorry for the delay at the delivery, but we had a big demand of cases at the time.

We were very surprise when we heard about the bottle of wine with bad taste. It is the first time that this has happened in our company. We apologise for this and be sure this will never happen again.

In reference to the cost of the original case, we are sending to you a voucher for the full value of the order. We enclose the latest catalogue with new products and special offers. We hope to receive a new order from you.

Please, contact us if you need any further information and we look forward to receiving your new order.

Yours sincerely,
Philippe Deval

2 Read the exam task below and the Examiner's marking scheme.

> You work for a market research company. One of your clients – a travel agent – has asked you to advise them on e-commerce. Look at the figures they supplied below on which you have already made some comments. Then, using all these comments, write your report.
>
> Write 120–140 words.

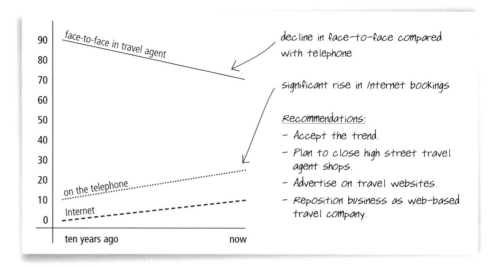

Examiner's marking scheme

Content	The report should deal with the two comments on the figures and the four comments of recommendation.
Organisation	The reason for writing should be made clear at the beginning of the report. Paragraphs and linking devices should be used to present the information clearly and logically.
Format	An appropriate format for a business-to-business report should be used.
Register	The register should be formal or neutral, and should be consistent.
Target reader	The travel agent should understand the points made about the changes in bookings, and the advice given.

Now read the sample answer. Has the writer has answered the question successfully?

Sample Report

Patagonia Travel Agency – E-commerce

The purpose of this report is to evaluate the current situation of e-commerce in Patagonia Travel Agency in connection with other traditional ways of running the business.

We have investigated it using some comments and figures that the company provided, analysing its operations from ten years ago to now.

We could see a sudden decline in face-to-face transactions from 90% to 70% approximately, due to the fact that customers have changed their attitudes and prefer other ways of operating. For example, telephone reservations have experienced an increase of 15% approximately and Internet booking has risen significantly.

As regards the market tendency, we suggest that the company should plan to close High Street shops. Meanwhile, we advise the company to change its business strategy and move gradually to a web-based travel agency.

sample speaking test

Find a partner to practise the different parts of the test.

Speaking Part 1: General questions (about 3 minutes)

Examiner   Hello. I'm (name) and this is my colleague (name). He/She is just going to listen to us. Could I have your mark sheets, please?

What's your name?
Where do you live?
Do you like living there?
Are you studying or do you work?
Do you have to travel far to work?
What are you going to do after your studies?
Would you like to work abroad?
What do you enjoy about your job?
What sort of job would you like to be doing in ten years?
Is it difficult to find a job in your field?

Thank you. That's the end of the first part of the test. In the next part you are each going to give a short presentation.

Speaking Part 2: Mini presentations/Short talk (about 6 minutes)

Examiner   I'm going to give each of you a choice of three topics. I'd like you to choose one of the topics and give a short presentation on it for about a minute. You will have about a minute to prepare for this and you can make notes if you wish while you prepare. After you have finished your talk, your partner will ask you a question.

All right? Here are your topics.

[Examiner hands each candidate a different topic card, and some paper and a pencil for making notes.]

Choose one of the topics to talk about. You can make notes.

[One minute's preparation time. Both candidates prepare their talks at the same time, separately.]

All right. Now, B, which topic have you chosen, A, B or C? ... Would you like to talk about what you think is important when ... [see Task Sheet 2, page 79]

[45 seconds to one minute]

Student B   ....

Thank you. Now, A, please ask B your question about his/her talk.

Student A/B   ....

Thank you. All right. Now, A, which topic have you chosen, A, B or C? ... Would you like to talk about what you think is important when ... [see Task Sheet 1, page 79]

[45 seconds to one minute]

Student A   ....

Thank you. Now, B, please ask A your question about his/her talk.

Student B/A   ....

Thank you.

Task Sheet 1 (Candidate A)

A

WHAT IS IMPORTANT WHEN ...?

Choosing the best candidate for a job

- qualifications
- experience
- •
- •

B

WHAT IS IMPORTANT WHEN ...?

Trying to motivate staff

- pay
- promotion opportunities
- •
- •

C

WHAT IS IMPORTANT WHEN ...?

Choosing a new office

- location
- environment
- •
- •

Task Sheet 2 (Candidate B)

A

WHAT IS IMPORTANT WHEN ...?

Choosing a location for a company

- size of local market
- efficiency of transport/communications
- •
- •

B

WHAT IS IMPORTANT WHEN ...?

Choosing a business leader

- vision
- experience
- •
- •

C

WHAT IS IMPORTANT WHEN ...?

Dealing with customers

- relationships
- quality of produce/service
- •
- •

Speaking Part 3: Collaborative task and discussion (about 5 minutes)

Examiner: Now in this part of the test, you are going to discuss something together.

[Examiner points to the card showing the task while giving the instructions below.]

You have about 30 seconds to read the task carefully, and then about three minutes to discuss and decide about it together. You should give reasons for your decisions and opinions. You don't need to write anything. Is that clear?

[Examiner places the card in front of the candidates.]

Your company needs to reduce its spending due to a slow-down in business. You have been asked to decide the cost areas which could be cut.
Discuss the situation together, and decide:
• whether to cut staff benefits, such as subsidised meals, travel allowances, free parking, etc.
• or to cut investment in promotional gifts and advertising.

I'm just going to listen and then ask you to stop after about three minutes. Please speak so that we can hear you.

Further questions
• Do you think customers need promotional gifts?
• Can we really see the benefits of advertising?
• What about cutting another area of costs, for example, research and development?
• Do you think staff would prefer to pay for their parking rather than risk losing business?
• What about the top managers taking a reduction in their salaries?
• What benefits would you look for with a new job?

key and tapescripts

unit 1

vocabulary

1
1 d	5 j	9 a
2 h	6 g	10 k
3 b	7 l	11 c
4 f	8 e	12 i

2 a Henry Ford
b Ray Kroc
c Akio Morita
d Ted Turner
e Sam Walton
f Michael Dell

3
R	C	H	E	U	A	C	I	O	J	N	P	W	T	A
E	V	I	G	Y	I	A	L	U	R	E	H	I	N	M
U	W	O	R	K	E	R	E	F	S	W	I	V	B	C
P	O	B	F	S	E	E	T	U	Y	U	N	K	L	R
I	E	D	S	F	R	E	E	L	A	N	C	E	W	S
C	M	V	G	E	N	R	D	F	E	M	O	F	I	K
Z	P	A	W	Y	S	C	B	I	L	I	M	P	G	I
B	L	E	N	E	M	P	L	O	Y	E	E	I	L	
P	O	N	O	E	C	D	Y	M	L	B	H	R	O	L
G	Y	T	M	A	U	V	S	E	R	V	I	C	E	S
R	E	N	P	U	R	J	W	N	L	E	P	M	T	N
O	R	G	A	N	I	S	A	T	I	O	N	Y	I	P
S	E	F	N	U	T	O	L	S	N	J	L	C	V	M
A	F	B	Y	D	Y	R	M	A	N	A	G	E	R	W

4 learning tips

noun – concept
organisation
management
creation

noun – people
organiser
communicator
manager

verb
communicate
manage
create

adjective
organised
communicative
creative

negatives
disorganised
uncommunicative
unmanageable
uncreative

reading

1 B	6 D	11 B
2 B	7 A	12 A
3 C	8 B	13 D
4 B	9 A	14 B
5 C	10 C	15 B

listening

1 B	4 C	7 A
2 B	5 C	
3 A	6 A	

tapescript

We are living in a time of change and I believe that everyone needs to be aware of how we can best cope with the challenges of the future. There are many scenarios, but here are some of my personal visions for the future – a future for a strong economy. We need to try to make it easier for people to find good jobs by giving them the education and training they need in order to succeed. It is a well-known fact that a successful working life usually begins with a good education. This is even more true as our economy changes.

Moving on to my next point. Getting and keeping a good job is not only the responsibility of the employee. Employers also need to play their part by offering help and encouragement. Employers have to be regularly reminded that they need to do more in order to keep their workers, for example, by ensuring that there are adequate opportunities for advancement. Central to this is a good programme of on-the-job training, one which allows and encourages people to achieve their potential.

If we look for a moment at the wider context, we can say that one of the great virtues of this country is the value we place on hard work and the respect we have for those who work hard. It is important that hard-working people see how their contributions have helped to make this country grow stronger and stronger. And, of course, this hard work must be rewarded. The financial benefits should guarantee everyone an acceptable standard of living.

Of course, financial benefits are not everything. We also need to make sure that our social welfare system continues to provide essential services such as health care and education. Finally, the end of one's working life should not be the beginning of worry and hardship. Employees should be encouraged to build up reserves for their retirement. With an ageing population, we need to be aware of the impact on pensions. This will inevitably cause strains on state budgets and people need to realise this and make appropriate plans.

When I look at the range of companies which operate in our economy, there are many emerging trends which I could mention. Here are just two. Firstly, organisations are becoming flatter, leaner and more flexible. Those companies which have taken out layers of management see many benefits. They are better able to keep up with technological advances and are more competitive. Secondly, the job market itself is changing. In the past, an employee could expect to spend a large part of his or her working life with one or two employers. Today, the job market, as well as the jobs themselves, require workers to be more mobile and more flexible. Again, we must ensure that a balance is maintained between the needs of our companies to make profit and the needs of their employees to lead fulfilled lives.

language in use

1
1 indirect	4 closed
2 open	5 closed
3 indirect	6 open

2 Suggested answers
1 How can people prepare for the future?
2 What do they need to become more aware of?
3 Do you think these changes will affect the world of work?
4 When did this trend start?
5 I'd like to know what the main changes for people in the world of work will be?
6 Do you see this as an inevitable trend?
7 Why have you specifically chosen this trend?

writing

1 d Bye / See you
2 a Yours faithfully
3 b Yours sincerely
4 c Best wishes / Regards / Best regards

fun and games

1 h	4 a	7 e
2 c	5 g	8 d
3 f	6 b	

unit 2

vocabulary

1
1 h	5 i	9 d
2 c	6 e	10 g
3 f	7 b	
4 a	8 j	

2
1 is headed
2 carries out
3 leads
4 are responsible
5 deals with
6 in charge
7 solves
8 organises
9 supported by
10 manage

3
1 competitive
2 strategies
3 team
4 customer
5 Analyses
6 conferences
7 reports
8 needs
9 launch
10 groups

4 learning tips
2 travel arrangements
3 market research
4 quality control
5 product information
6 support staff
7 team members
8 information systems

reading

1 B		4 C
2 A		5 A
3 D		6 A

listening

1 B	5 A
2 B	6 C
3 C	7 C
4 C	

tapescript

Good evening, everyone and thank you all for staying on this evening. I'd like to get straight down to the issue in hand. As I'm sure you're well aware, the current increase in business has put a severe strain on our company structure. Increases in business are precisely what we need, but coping with them presents certain, shall we say, challenges. So, I'd like to look at how we can best face the future. This will involve major changes; and, as change is sometimes painful, I propose to introduce these through a measured programme of modifications.

The first thing to be said is that our current hierarchy is not really well adapted to market conditions. As we've all seen over the last couple of years, we're expected to respond ever more quickly to clients' orders. In my opinion, the best way to do this is by introducing a flatter structure. Too many layers of managers and supervisors slow down the whole process. This is a general issue that we need to act on, but one that is particularly serious in the area of sales. So we need to remove some of the bottlenecks caused by having too many departments involved in the same process. That's one area that we'll need to focus on.

Next, I have noted that the Purchasing Department has been very active – however, not always in the best interests of the company. We must be able to take advantage of the opportunities provided by business-to-business purchasing by buying more of our standard materials on-line. We need to embrace the new technologies, not stick to our old ways, simply because they're more comfortable. With our new IT system, we have the technology to make significant savings by buying on-line. In fact, more and more of our existing suppliers can provide us with on-line purchasing. I will therefore be bringing in an e-purchasing consultant, someone who can advise us on the opportunities, as well as the risks, of buying on-line. This person will then work with our team to analyse our current procedures and advise the department on streamlining them. I'm sure we can both simplify our purchasing procedures and make savings by using the opportunities to buy on-line.

Moving on. The next area is finance. I've decided to bring in a new controller to work alongside our current Finance Director. As you all know, Greg Barnes is due to retire next year and we need to consider how to replace him. This, therefore, will be the first step and I hope that this will lead to a smooth handover when the time comes for Greg to step down.

Finally, a few words about our IT department in general. I know that the last few years have seen radical changes in the way that we do our business. And the IT department has come to play an increasingly central role in our activities. First of all, I'd like to assure you that IT will continue to be a support function in this company. We are not an IT business, but we do need to maximise the benefits of the electronic revolution.

I've already spoken about purchasing, but I would like to see this company at the cutting edge of new developments. At present, I sense quite a lot of opposition to new trends, and this will need to be addressed. Therefore, I'm proposing to set up an inter-departmental working group, consisting of all heads, to look at how we can improve our ways of sharing information. Of course, this need not be limited to computer media. We also need to introduce more information meetings, where we can exchange ideas, opinions and details about how to improve our ways of working. The objective of this exercise will be to establish proposals for a new company structure twelve months from now. At that point we will look again at how the company is organised …

language in use

1
1 PS2		4 PS1
2 PC1		5 PC2
3 PS1		6 PC2

2
1 review
2 doesn't always involve
3 leads
4 does the current situation show
5 're experiencing
6 means
7 has
8 reports
9 works
10 're noticing
11 're planning
12 don't foresee
13 don't normally happen
14 am expecting
15 share

writing

1	b	3	c
2	d	4	a

fun and games

Suggested answers

1 the one before, i.e. the previous manager

2 He resigns.

unit 3

vocabulary

1

1	d	5	e
2	g	6	a
3	b	7	h
4	f	8	c

2
1 ticket
2 tip
3 check in
4 seat belt
5 receipt
6 excess baggage
7 hand luggage
8 aisle
9 reservation
10 book

3
a frequent flyer
b overnight flight
c time zone
d health risk
e global economy
f jet lag
g a perk of the job
h cramped seat

4 learning tips

adjective + noun
overnight flight
global economy
cramped seat

noun + noun
time zone
health risk

language in use

1
1 ✓
2 Book as early as **possible** to get the best seat.
3 ✓
4 ✓
5 If you want to get to the city centre, public transport is **much quicker** than a taxi in the rush hour.
6 Teleconferencing is (much) **more** convenient than travelling to overseas meetings.

7 The **less** tired you are, the more efficient you'll be in the meeting.
8 The **simplest** precaution is to cover your health by suitable insurance.

2
1 harder
2 longer
3 more time-consuming
4 smaller
5 as slow
6 the most expensive
7 less
8 less
9 the worst

reading

1	D	4	B	7	A
2	A	5	C		
3	D	6	B		

listening

Call 1
1 Yellow fever
2 Wednesday
3 658736
4 every weekday

Call 2
5 567G
6 laptop
7 Europe
8 booklet

Call 3
9 Meyer
10 ESP3598
11 New York
12 two suitcases

tapescript

Call 1

This is the vaccination helpline. The following information is for travellers intending to visit destinations in East Africa. This message deals with five diseases: yellow fever, typhoid, tetanus, polio and cholera.

A certificate of vaccination is required against yellow fever in some countries. Travellers who are not in possession of a valid certificate will not be granted entry. Vaccination clinics take place on Monday and Wednesday afternoons.

Vaccination against typhoid is recommended, but is not a requirement. We are not offering this clinic at present. For further information, call 01205 658736.

The Department of Health recommends regular booster vaccinations in the event of injuries which may give rise to tetanus. Clinics are on Tuesday mornings only.

Polio vaccine is recommended for long-term travellers, staying more than six

months, to areas which have a high incidence of the disease such as developing countries. Clinics are held every weekday in our Southampton Row practice.

Cholera vaccine offers poor protection against the disease and is no longer recommended by the Department of Health or the World Health Organisation.

Please ensure that you arrange your vaccinations in good time.

This is the end of the message.

Call 2

A ... Please leave a message after the beep.

B Oh, hello, my name is Jane Ronson. I have just received an annual travel insurance policy issued by your company for Dirk Meyer. The number is 567G. But there's a problem with the cover. On my application form, we asked for the following cover: a Toshiba laptop and winter sports worldwide. The policy document that you sent specifies a Dell laptop and winter sports in Europe only. Um, please could you send a new policy with the correct cover? Also, we asked for a booklet explaining procedures in the event of a claim. I'm afraid you forgot to send that. Thank you.

Call 3

A AirSearch, good morning. You're talking to Mary. How can I help you?

B Good morning. I'm trying to track down two bags which didn't arrive yesterday.

A OK. If you can give me some details.

B Fine.

A First of all, do you have a reference number?

B Yes, it's KLJ567348922.

A Just a moment. Sorry, it's not on my computer. Let me take the details now.

B OK.

A Can you give me the passenger's name, please?

B Yes, it's Dirk Meyer. That's M-E-Y-E-R.

A OK, and where was Mr Meyer travelling from?

B From Madrid.

A And do you have the flight number?

B Yes, it was ESP3598.

A Right. I've got it now. That was to New York via Amsterdam, which is where the luggage got delayed. Unfortunately, none of the bags made the connection. How many bags are missing?

B Two suitcases.

A OK, the latest information I have is that the bags will be with you later today.

B Do you know when?

A Should be by five o'clock.

B Good. Thanks a lot.

A You're welcome. Bye.

B Bye.

writing

1 j
2 h, b
3 e, a
4 d, i

fun and games

1 Tanzania
2 Sweden, Norway and Denmark
3 Ireland
4 Reykjavik
5 Brussels
6 Arabic
7 Poland
8 California
9 nine
10 Singapore

unit 4

vocabulary

1 1 review
2 bankruptcies
3 raise
4 profits
5 cutting
6 reduce
7 staff
8 collapse
9 generated
10 redundancies
11 improvement
12 increase

2 2 g   5 d
3 c   6 a
4 f   7 b

3 Across   Down
4 competition   1 optimistic
5 retailer   2 similar
9 advantage   3 entered
11 slowdown   6 failure
12 launch   7 variety
    8 boring
    10 global

4 learning tips

beautiful   inclusive
attractive   industrial
optional   valuable
remarkable   expressive
harmful   competitive

reading

1 A   4 B
2 E   5 F
3 C

listening

1 B   4 B
2 A   5 C
3 C   6 A

tapescript

Welcome to the AGM. Let me briefly introduce myself. My name is Carola da Silva and I am currently chairman of Pharma Diagnostics. However, as many of you know I have now had five eventful years on the Board; so my duties will be completed at the end of the month. Therefore, one of the tasks for this meeting will be to elect a new chairman. But more on that later. The business of the day is shown on your agendas, which all of you should have received, together with the minutes from the last meeting. As you can see from your programme, there are four items of business: firstly, approval of the minutes from last year's AGM; secondly, the approval of the accounts; thirdly, the changes to the constitution of the Board; and finally, the re-appointment of Zapata and Meribel to prepare our accounts next year. After the conclusion of the main business, we will deal with Any Other Business.

Let me briefly explain the documents that you will find in your file. Firstly, the Profit and Loss statement for the year just gone. This year is consolidated and presents the results for our worldwide operations. However, the Asian companies, which are totally independent are not shown in this document. Secondly, the balance sheet as of 31st December. This shows the figure for the company's European operations; so it excludes other territories.

Just a word on the procedures for voting. This is really for those who have not attended our AGM before. According to our constitution, voting will be by a show of hands and decisions will be by majority voting. For a motion to be approved, it needs a minimum of 50% of the total votes including those who

cannot be here today. In fact, there are 453 registered voters here today and we have received the voting intentions of another 64.

Moving on. As I am due to stand down as Chairman on 31st January, we will need to appoint three new members for your Board, in other words, a chairman and two other members. You have all received details of the seven candidates, standing for election. However, Markus Obermeier has since withdrawn his nomination. So, we will be making a choice from six candidates for three posts.

The accounts have been prepared by the firm of Zapata and Merribel. This was their first year in this role. The final point on the agenda will be to vote on their re-appointment.

I'd now like to invite you to contribute items for the AOB slot. If we could spend ten minutes or so collecting any issues for the afternoon session. I see we have some hands. Yes, the gentleman in the red shirt. Could you stand up and give us the item you'd like us to consider?

language in use

1 a ✓
b How long **have you used** Zapata and Merribel as your accountants?
c This year's results show that the company **has made** an unexpected profit.
d ✓
e When **did you revise** the budget?

2

A **Have** you **seen** last year's end-of-year report yet?
B Yes, it **arrived** on my desk yesterday.
A And what **did** you **think**?
B I must admit, the results **were** better than I anticipated. The company **didn't do** so badly in Europe.
A Yes, but we **made** some terrible losses in South America.
B Well, the results are broadly in line with what I **expected**. The subsidiary there **has suffered** terribly as a result of the economic downturn. And things **have deteriorated** even further recently.
A That's true. I **had** a discussion with the Finance Director last week and he **told** me that he **felt** really pessimistic about the next five years.
B I know, but **have you ever met** a Finance Director who **wasn't** pessimistic? I know I haven't.

writing

Model answer

> **Report on quarter: January–March**
>
> The January figures show a good increase on last year. The main reason for our growth was the very cold weather, which attracted a lot of visitors. February sales were down considerably. In particular, sales were affected by the opening of the new Playland facility. Their special discounts attracted a lot of new customers away from us. In addition, we suffered from an overall downturn in consumer spending. In March we just missed our target. The figures show a good increase on last year.
>
> The profit figures are disappointing, although we had two good months. The high costs during the period led to poor actual profit. We therefore need to review all forecast costs ahead of the next quarter to identify areas where we can make savings.

fun and games

> The **Annual General Meeting** was held on 24 September. After the Chairman presented the agenda, he asked if there was **Any Other Business**.
>
> During the meeting, the Chairman presented the **Profit and Loss** statement for **Quarter 1 / the first quarter**. It showed that while sales had risen to **one point four million dollars**, costs had risen by **approximately five per cent**. The result was a very poor **Return On Investment**. The Chairman said he didn't expect the **business** to improve next year.
>
> When the **Chief Finance Officer** announced that the company would not be paying out a dividend, the shareholders demanded an explanation. There were angry scenes when it was announced that the directors had received pay rises of about **ten per cent per annum** for the last six years.

unit 5

vocabulary

1 1 e-mail
2 office gossip
3 face-to-face
4 post
5 fax
6 meeting
7 in-house magazine
8 noticeboard
9 memo

2 1 advise; advisory / advisable
2 confidence; confide
3 privacy; privatise
4 respond; responsive
5 revolution; revolutionary
6 sensitivity; sensitise
7 urgency; urge
8 use; useable / useless

3 1 e noun + noun
2 c noun + noun
3 a adjective + noun
4 b adjective + noun
5 f adjective + noun
6 d adjective + noun

4 1 invaluable tool
2 fax machine
3 computer screen
4 important documents
5 imminent arrival
6 paperless office

5 learning tips

countable
document
office
network

uncountable
correspondence
cyberspace
staff

proper
Mexico
Microsoft
Wednesday

reading

01 FOR
02 BEEN
03 THE
04 IF
05 CORRECT
06 AT
07 YOU
08 CORRECT
09 CAREFUL
10 DOWN
11 CORRECT
12 CORRECT

listening

1 1 G   4 F
   2 E   5 A
   3 H

2 1 E   4 D
   2 B   5 F
   3 A

tapescript

1

1

A Hi, Peter. You're looking very well. How was your holiday?

B Absolutely marvellous. Great weather, wonderful food.

A Sounds like you had a really tremendous time.

B And when are you off?

A In a couple of weeks. I can't wait.

2

I've divided this talk into three main parts. First, we'll look at the markets. Then I want to address the current staffing arrangements; and finally I'd like to consider the challenges for next year. I aim to talk for about fifteen minutes. If you have any questions, I'd be grateful if you could wait till the end.

3

So let me just outline the plan. First, I'd like to give you a brief description of the company, so that you have a better idea of where the position of Network Co-ordinator fits in. Then I'd like to find out more about your track record to date. It looks like you have a lot of relevant experience. In particular, I'd like to look at your responsibilities in your last job. And then you'll have a chance to ask me any questions about the position. Is that OK?

4

A I'm afraid I can't accept your current offer. We have done a few sums and we feel that for the quantity that we are interested in, your price is too high.

B OK, then we shall need to look again at our figures. But before we do, could you give me an idea of how you reached your proposed buying price?

A Yes, of course. The calculation was based on an order of 50,000 items to be supplied in twelve regular instalments.

5

I'm delighted to be able to tell you all that we have had another excellent month. In fact, sales have reached an all-time high and we seem to have managed to reduce our costs slightly. Of course, this has not been easy. So, I would like to congratulate you all on your performance. So, that's the background to this meeting. I'd also like to ask Klaus Hoffman to fill in the details for us …

2

1

A I don't know why you can't just send the information in a letter. I mean I'm sure that Janice will want to have a written record of the decision.

B Yes, of course she will. But as this is a sensitive matter I think I should call her.

A And what about putting it in writing?

B No, I don't think so at this stage.

A OK, if you feel that that's the best way, then go ahead and do that.

2

The key question is how to provide our own people with opportunities to develop their own knowledge and skills. As you know, we already have an extensive collection of materials for self-study; but I believe we need to increase these resources. So, over the last few weeks, I have collected a lot of information on e-learning provided by different suppliers. After I have collated all the details, I suggest that we sit down together to review the different offers. Can we just look in our diaries to fix a date for that?

3

A I spoke to Susan on the phone earlier today about the figures. Naturally she was quite shocked.

B Yes, I can imagine they came as quite a surprise. So, what's next?

A Well, we discussed how best to inform everyone about the results. Susan's suggestion was to call a meeting.

B I don't think a meeting at this stage would be the right forum.

A Yes, I agree entirely. So I finally persuaded her to give a short talk to everyone to outline the current position.

B Good.

A And she agreed to talk to us next Monday at two o'clock.

4

A Oh dear, I think I've deleted the message.

B Don't worry, you can always retrieve it from trash. If you click on 'trash' here, you'll find it.

A Oh! There it is. Good. That's a relief!

B So now you know what to do.

A Yes, thanks. So, I'll send him a confirmation about the meeting right away.

B Yes, and please send a copy to me. And don't forget to attach the file to the message.

5

A How are you going to present the results?

B I was thinking of putting them into a memo to send round to everyone, but now I'm having second thoughts.

A Why's that?

B Well, first of all it's much too long. So, I plan to put the information into a report. Then the tables and the graphics will look more dynamic.

A But you'll need to send it to a lot of people.

B I know, but I think it needs to be in the right format. I'll decide later on how to get it to people.

language in use

1

agenda	C	information	U
benefit	C	memo	C
client	C	report	C
confidentiality	U	research	U
machine	C	turnover	U
gossip	U	work	U

2
Suggested answer

Dear Pierre

I have received **an e-mail** from Magda in which she asks for **advice** about the forthcoming presentation that she has to give at the end-of-year meeting. I couldn't give her any **information** and suggested that she **makes contact** with Stasek, who is organising the whole event. If you have **time**, perhaps you could do some **research** for her. If you could send her **a short message** and some guidelines, I am sure she would be very happy to hear from you.

Finally, please could you let me know as soon as possible if you have received the **minutes** from the last meeting. I haven't and would like to see a copy before preparing the **agenda** for our next meeting.

I look forward to seeing you again in the Hague.

Regards

Simone

writing
Model answers
1

From: Peter Brown
To: Customer Relations Manager
Subject: Late delivery of order IF435

Dear Monica

The above order was placed at the beginning of July and I was guaranteed delivery within a maximum of four weeks. This is now urgently required as I have customers waiting for their order. Please get back to me with an expected delivery date.

Regards

Peter Brown

Store Manager

2

From: Monica de Vries
To: Peter Brown
Subject: Re order IF435

Dear Peter

I apologise for the late delivery of your July order. The reason is that our suppliers in Japan are having problems getting the memory chips.

As soon as I have a firm delivery date, I'll contact you.

Regards

Monica de Vries

Customer Relations Manager

fun and games

The man on the left has positive body language. He's leaning forward in his chair, maintaining eye contact and smiling. The woman looks bored and distracted. She isn't contributing to the conversation and probably isn't listening to what is being said. The man on the right also has positive body language. From his open hands, it is clear that he's accepting what the man is saying to him.

unit 6

vocabulary

1

1 d	4 a	7 i
2 b	5 h	8 c
3 e	6 f	9 g

2

b endanger	f ensure
c legislation	g machinery
d protective	h Prolonged
e adjustable	i slippery

3

M	V	T	A	D	J	U	S	T	A	B	L	E	T	A
F	H	J	G	Y	I	N	M	V	T	E	I	J	H	M
V	A	D	R	O	Z	O	N	E	S	N	E	V	J	C
Q	Z	B	F	S	E	B	U	V	Z	T	M	F	B	S
J	A	D	S	F	R	S	E	L	I	N	S	L	I	P
D	R	A	D	I	A	T	I	O	N	M	L	F	I	O
A	D	B	C	U	T	R	B	A	J	S	I	P	G	I
S	M	E	S	N	E	U	P	L	U	Y	P	E	I	G
A	P	N	T	E	C	C	Y	T	R	I	P	R	O	L
F	Y	T	R	A	U	T	S	E	Y	V	E	C	E	S
E	N	D	A	N	G	E	R	N	L	E	R	M	T	N
T	R	G	I	O	J	D	B	S	J	N	V	V	I	P
Y	F	E	N	V	S	P	M	T	O	K	M	D	W	N

4 learning tips

a	P	e	P
b	A	f	A
c	P	g	P
d	P		

reading

1	B	4	A
2	C	5	A
3	D	6	C

listening

1	B	5	C
2	A	6	A
3	C	7	C
4	B	8	A

tapescript

A Marina, you've been involved with health and safety issues at a number of large international companies and recently you've been working on a project to analyse European accident statistics. Your report is about to be published. What exactly do these statistics on workplace accidents show us?

B Well, first of all, let me explain the starting point for our calculations. The measure that we use is based on the accident rate per 100,000 workers.

A Right.

B And then we make a distinction between fatal and non-fatal accidents. So, that's the basic framework.

A OK.

B Right, if we look first of all at fatal injuries, we can see that the rate is 1.05.

A That's per 100,000 workers.

B Yes, exactly. And this is contrasted with the non-fatal accident rate …

A … which I expect is much higher.

B Yes, of course. The corresponding figure is 648.1.

A And how many accidents are we talking about in each category?

B The number of fatal accidents last year was 295 in total; and that represented an increase of 75 on the previous year.

A I suppose that these figures increase year on year.

B No, not at all. The number and rate of fatal injury to workers generally fell during the 1990s. So, the increase in the rate last year was quite unexpected.

A Any specific reason?

B No, but we haven't completed our analysis yet. But what we can say is that the numbers and rates of fatal injury are higher in all the main industrial sectors, especially agriculture, manufacturing, construction sectors, and the service sector.

A And can you say what specifically caused the accidents?

B Well, we can see substantial increases in the number of fatal injuries due to workers being hit by moving or falling objects, hit by a vehicle, or being trapped by something collapsing or overturning. But that is what we see each year, namely that the most common kinds of fatal accidents are caused by falling from a height, being struck by a moving vehicle or being struck by moving or falling objects.

A I see.

B Now, if we look at non-fatal injuries, we can see a similar downward trend during the first half of the 90s.

A With an increase in the second part?

B Actually, no. Since the mid-90s, the number of reported injuries has remained more or less stable.

A I see. And do you think that this trend will continue?

B Too early to say. But we certainly hope so.

A And are there significant differences between men and women?

B Our figures show that overall, in other words for all kinds of accidents, the rates of both fatal and non-fatal injury are higher in men than women. And the highest rates of fatal injury in terms of age are for older male workers.

A Any other significant differences based on age?

B Yes and no. First of all, our evidence shows that there's no difference in rates of non-fatal injuries for younger and older workers. However, our figures show that the rate of less serious injury is higher in young men if we compare them with older men.

In fact, workers in the first few months with their employer have the highest rate of injury; and workers on a low number of weekly hours have substantially higher rates of injury than those working longer hours, and the rate gets lower as the number of weekly hours increases.

A We've mainly talked about risk of death or injury. Where is there the lowest risk?

B Very difficult to answer. Although, there are clearly industries which have a higher incidence of injuries, the main cause of accidents is through not having sufficient knowledge to do the job properly. This means that if you know how to do the job, your risk should be lower. I think that this is what our research shows. The more you train people, the lower the risk of an accident.

language in use

1

modal	meanings
can	ability
can't	inability/impossibility
could	prediction when there is doubt
may	possibility/permission
must	obligation
mustn't	prohibition
should	advice

2 Suggested answers

1	can't	5	can
2	should	6	could
3	must	7	mustn't
4	should	8	May

writing

Model answer

Accident report
From: Miroslav Cernik
To: Health and Safety Department

I am a car body sprayer and have worked in the paint shop for more than five years.

On 14 January at 11.30, I was working in the paint workshop when I had accident. While I was carrying materials to my workplace, I fell on the floor, which was wet and slippery. I went to the company nurse, who treated my arm. She told me that it was broken and that I had to go home.

I have been off work for more than a week. As a result of the accident I am unable to help at home. I visit the physiotherapist every day, who treats me. I would be grateful if you could investigate my claim as soon as possible.

fun and games

1 Not drinking water
Staff only
Mobile phones prohibited
No dogs (except guide dogs)
No smoking

2 First aid post
Emergency exit
Emergency eye wash
Fire extinguisher

unit 7

vocabulary

1
1 j   5 d   9 h
2 f   6 i   10 c
3 g   7 e
4 a   8 b

2
1 f   5 a   9 h
2 b   6 g   10 e
3 d   7 i
4 j   8 c

3 Across   **Down**
1 requirements   1 recruiters
4 expertise   2 qualified
6 openings   3 employees
8 sort   5 board
9 agencies   7 shortage
10 skills
11 attracting

4 learning tips

a ✓
b Each year we recruit about **a
  hundred and twenty** new
  employees.
c ✓
d Management salaries start at
  between forty and fifty **thousand
  dollars.**
e More than a **million units** come off
  the production line each year.

reading

01 CORRECT   07 TOTAL
02 TO   08 BY
03 AT   09 CORRECT
04 WILL   10 IT
05 CORRECT   11 EVEN
06 BE   12 THE

listening

1 B   4 B   7 B
2 C   5 A   8 B
3 A   6 C

tapescript

A Fabiella, your company has built up
  an enormous resource for training.
  When did you get involved with
  Global Training?

B I started off as a trainer myself
  working within the human resources
  department of a large multinational
  organisation. While I was there, I soon
  realised that companies were not
  really well served with quality
  information about external training
  products. And in today's competitive
  environment, training is critical for
  success. For example, it can improve
  job performance, it can increase sales,
  it can even protect employees. But
  these things don't just happen.
  Training has to be planned,
  encouraged and implemented. So our
  aim at Global Training is to provide a
  complete service for companies that
  want to organise training, and trainers
  that have the skills to design and
  deliver training programmes.

A So how does it work?

B Well, we are involved in three main
  areas. Firstly, there are the training
  courses themselves; that's the main
  service we provide; bringing together
  clients and trainers. Secondly, we
  provide training products; and finally,
  we can help a client to run a training
  course or conference anywhere in the
  world by providing information about
  facilities.

A So, if someone comes to you with a
  training request, how is the enquiry
  processed?

B We hold very extensive databases of
  courses, of trainers, of consultants, of
  training seminars and workshops, of
  computer labs and classrooms, and of
  keynote speakers. Of course, we get
  requests not only from the corporate
  world, but also from the public sector
  and from professional associations.
  So, if someone from a company
  background, an HR manager or a
  training manager, comes to us with a
  specific training request, we would
  identify the specific objectives for
  their training programme. That has to
  be the starting point for any course.
  This is usually carried out by a
  detailed interview together with an
  in-depth questionnaire. The results are
  then put into a course proposal. If the
  client is happy with what we propose,
  then we would move on to the next
  stage.

A Which is …?

B Which is to look for trainers with the
  expertise to run the course.

A I see. You said that you get requests
  outside the corporate world.

B Mmm, yes, about 25% of our
  business comes from the public
  sector – schools, colleges, etc. and
  from professional organisations for
  doctors, architects, and so on.

A So, what areas can you organise
  training for?

B We cover a very wide range. To
  enable professionals to search our
  database, our training is categorised
  under 50 headings.

A Can you give me an example?

B Of course, let me give you examples
  from different sectors. If we take the
  public sector, we can provide courses
  for adults in basic reading, writing and
  maths skills, and general job skills. At
  the other end of the spectrum, we
  run courses for professionals in
  manufacturing who need to improve
  their skills in computer design,
  materials management, and
  production planning. So, we would
  receive an enquiry for a particular
  type of training, usually something
  that is specified in one of our
  categories. And we would discuss the
  specific requirements with the client,
  as I explained earlier.

A And once the course objectives and
  content are agreed, you would search
  your database to find a trainer.

B A suitable trainer. That is very
  important. Apart from subject
  knowledge, our trainers have
  experience of all delivery media,
  including instructor led on-line
  courses, computer based training,
  videos, and so on.

A So, let's imagine that the client has
  agreed the course content and the
  profile of the trainer, what happens
  next?

B Next, we need to find the right
  location for the training. If the client
  doesn't have their own premises, we
  search for a suitable venue and that
  can be anywhere in the world. Again,
  our database has details of facilities
  that are available for training and
  conference-related events.

A So, if I wanted to run a course in the
  Bahamas, could you find me a
  suitable location?

B Yes, in fact we just organised a
  conference for a major client out
  there a couple of months ago. There
  were 350 delegates who stayed for a
  five-day sales meeting. The venue
  provided a conference hall, complete
  with small seminar rooms, a library,
  recreation rooms, and lounges.

Participants were housed in five hotels all with the use of a gymnasium, and many other recreational facilities.

A Sounds ideal.

B Yes, it was a great success. Of course, not all the requests involve such grand plans. At the other extreme, we get requests for training products. For example, a client running a language training course might like some material as follow-up to the course. Again, our database will identify suitable materials.

A Well, you've already built up Global Training into a very successful company. Good luck for the future.

B Thanks.

language in use

1 also A
although C
however C
in addition A
on the other hand C
not only … but also A
moreover A
though C
too A
whereas C
while C

2 1 not only
2 but also
3 Although
4 also
5 While
6 In addition
7 Whereas
8 too
9 Though
10 Moreover
11 on the other hand

writing

1 1 a   4 b   7 d   10 b
2 d   5 c   8 a
3 a   6 a   9 b

2 8, 6, 1, 3, 9, 10, 4, 5, 7, 2

fun and games

Suggested answers

+++   1, 7, 9
++   6, 8, 10, 11
+   2, 3, 4, 12
x   5, 13

unit 8

vocabulary

1 1 b   5 b
2 b   6 b
3 c   7 a
4 a   8 c

2 **noun – people**
competitor
advertiser
consumer

verb
compete
advertise
attract
appeal
consume
desire

adjective
competitive
commercial
attractive
appealing
desirable

negative
non-competitive
non-commercial
unattractive
unappealing
undesirable

3 attractive
desirability
competitors
consumers
appeal
advertising

4 1 series
2 full-page; half-page
3 single; mass
4 convinced
5 endorsement
6 listing; display
7 potential; actual
8 agency; print

5 **learning tips**
image
public image
to improve your public image
market
financial / property / falling market
to spot a gap in the market
to come on to the market
market leader / share / value
advertise
advertisement (advert / ad)
a TV advert / a job ad
to advertise on TV / in a newspaper
advertising campaign / agency

language in use

1 will be queuing
2 're going to talk about
3 'll cut out
4 is appearing
5 'll discuss
6 'll be
7 'm going to take
8 'm starting
9 will be
10 are you going to start
11 'll find out
12 'll have spent

reading

1 B   6 B   11 B
2 C   7 A   12 C
3 A   8 C   13 D
4 B   9 D   14 B
5 C   10 A   15 B

listening

Conversation 1
1 Peterson
2 Mobile
3 18th May
4 Household Goods
Conversation 2
5 Sales
6 Portugal
7 8678 9887
8 morning
Conversation 3
9 Recruitment (plus)
10 Spare
11 Care
12 Thursday

tapescript

Conversation 1

A Hello. This is Trade and Exchange. I'm afraid there's no one here to take your call. Please leave your name and telephone number, and a short message. If you wish to place an ad, please tell us what it is, under what heading you'd like it to appear and when you'd like the ad to appear. Please speak clearly after the beep.

B Hello, um, my name is Geoffrey Peterson, that's P-E-T-E-R-S-O-N. Um, my home telephone number is 01456 768891, um, or you can get me on my mobile, which is 0861 3557884. Um, and I'd like to place an ad in Monday's edition – that's um … the 16th … no, sorry, the 18th May, under the heading of Household Goods. Thanks. Bye.

Conversation 2

A Timeshare International. How can I help you?

B I'd like to discuss advertising in your magazine.

A Just a moment, I'll put you through to Sales. Who shall I say is calling?

B Sally Jacobs.

A Just a moment, Ms Jacobs …

C Sales and Advertising. Dawn Morell speaking.

B Hello, this is Sally Jacobs. I'd like to advertise a property in your magazine.

C Of course. Can I just ask if it is in the UK or abroad?

B It's in Portugal.

C In that case can I get my colleague David Miles to call you back? He deals with all our non-UK promotions.

B Fine. My number is 020 8678 9887.

C I've got that. He'll call back later this morning.

B That will be fine. Thanks. Bye.

C Bye.

Conversation 3

A Daily Herald. Classified. Tracey speaking.

B I'd like to speak to someone about a mistake in my ad.

A Can I just ask which section it was in?

B It was in yesterday's Recruitment section.

A Just a moment. I'll put you through.

C Katie speaking. How can I help you?

B This is Manfred Becker speaking. I placed an ad in your Recruitment plus section yesterday.

C Was it a standard ad or a display?

B I think you called it semi-display.

C And is there a problem?

B There certainly is. In the ad it said Customer Spare Assistant. It was meant to be for a Customer Care Assistant!

C I do apologise for that. Was the rest of the ad as specified?

B Yes, but this was in the headline.

C Mm, I understand. We'll run the ad for you again at no cost.

B Thank you. That'll be next Thursday?

C That's right.

B That's fine.

C Once again, Mr Becker. I do apologise.

B That's okay. Goodbye.

C Goodbye.

writing
Model answer

Dear Ms Berlot

Thank you for your recent **enquiry about advertising** in our monthly magazine 'The Great Outdoors'.

'The Great Outdoors' is one of the UK's most popular walking magazines and, **as you can see from** the enclosed readership figures, it **reaches / is read by / covers** a high percentage of the UK market. I **am also enclosing**:
• a current **issue / copy** of the magazine
• an advertising **rate** card.

The **deadline for** copy for the next issue is 5 June.

Please **(don't hesitate to) contact / get in touch with me** if **you require / need any further** information.

Yours **sincerely**
D Cartwright
Advertising Manager

fun and games

1 f	A	5 b	D
2 a	F	6 g	H
3 e	B	7 h	C
4 d	E	8 c	G

unit 9

vocabulary

1
2 j		5 h		8 i	
3 g		6 b		9 c	
4 a		7 e		10 d	

2 Across
3 domestic
4 overseas
7 global
8 buy
9 launch
11 headquarters
12 enter

Down
2 distributor
5 set up
6 dealer
10 agent

3
1 for		5 into	
2 up		6 up	
3 into		7 out	
4 up		8 up	

4 learning tips
a Look at
b Look up
c Look into
d look for
e Look after

reading

1
01 A		07 BE	
02 THE		08 BEING	
03 WITH		09 CORRECT	
04 THIS		10 THAN	
05 FOR		11 MIDDLE	
06 THROUGH		12 CORRECT	

2
1 E		4 F	
2 A		5 B	
3 D			

listening

1
1 E		4 F	
2 G		5 D	
3 B			

2
1 D		4 G	
2 E		5 A	
3 B			

tapescript

1

1 It's our job to get the products to the customers. We deal with a range of manufacturers. Of course, we make sure they are not direct competitors and then we use our national and local networks to deliver the products when the customers want them.

2 I'm based in Head Office. I look after all our foreign customers. Gradually, we've been extending our customer base. We usually do this through agents in the local markets. I've got a small team which deals with all the necessary licenses and permits you need to trade overseas.

3 It's our job to help support our national companies. This means organising trade delegations. Together with the Ministry of Trade we set up five or six a year. We also provide local intelligence in the commercial sector. For example, a company wanting to export can contact us for a list of agents or distributors.

4 My company set up a local office five years ago. Initially, the General Manager was appointed from Head Office but now there's a new policy to use local staff. So I'm the first local manager to run the branch.

5 We were taken over two years ago. At the time, I was the Sales Manager of a local company called Titan. We've now been renamed Photon Inc and I've been promoted to Area Sales Manager. This means I cover a much bigger market – not just this local area but several other countries in the region.

2

1 The biggest issue for us is making sure we have the right products in stock. You know, we order from our suppliers in good time to meet our customer's demand but things often go wrong. They get shipped to the wrong depot or there's some sort of strike. No, that's our biggest headache actually, getting the goods to the customers on time.

2 One of the challenges facing me is to get the quote right. The currency fluctuations, especially over the last few months, have made it very difficult. In these days of the Internet, there's a lot more transparency. Customers can even check how much their competitors are being charged.

3 We have found that there are very different ways of doing business. Here we spend much longer talking to our customers – we know everything about them, their families – everything. The head office staff are not used to giving this time. They just want to arrive, negotiate and sign the contract.

4 I think my biggest problem is helping our companies to deal with all the forms – you know the export licences, special permits, and so on. It's quite complex but we are able to advise them on how to get through all these steps.

5 For us what we find really difficult is explaining what it's like here – you know the market and the special needs we have. We need the chance for Head Office to visit us and for us to visit them. Only in this way will we really understand each other's needs.

language in use

1 If we set up a local subsidiary, we'd hire local staff.
2 If you visit the local embassy, you'll meet the commercial officer.
3 If we acquired AFB, our sales would double.
4 If international business increases, there will be more travel delays.
5 If we developed our export markets, we'd need English language expertise.
6 If there are public holidays abroad, the telephones are much quieter.
7 If we recruit a local branch manager, he / she will have to speak English.
8 If we don't / Unless we find an agent, we'll delay entry to the market.
9 If we don't / Unless we get a permit, we'll have to cancel the transport.
10 If I were you, I'd visit the subsidiary myself.

writing

1
1 b	5 a	9 b
2 d	6 b	10 b
3 c	7 b	11 d
4 c	8 c	

2 5, 6, 7, 9, 4, 1, 10, 8, 3, 2, 11

fun and games

1 g English, Maori
2 i English
3 e English
4 f Japanese
5 c Danish
7 h Arabic
8 j English, Welsh
9 b English, French
10 d Greek

unit 10

vocabulary

1
1 c	4 d
2 a	5 e
3 b	

2
1 We negotiated late into the night.
2 They invoiced us before delivery.
3 The price was discounted by nearly 15%.
4 They exhibited their products on the main stand.
5 We will demonstrate the new product later today.
6 Our customers were highly/very satisfied with our new model.
7 We are going to replace the goods damaged in transit.
8 Good sales people need to learn how to prioritise their calls.

3
1 stand	5 placed
2 leads	6 form
3 enquiry	7 close
4 prospects	8 delay

4 learning tips
1 inefficient
2 unsuccessful
3 unreliable
4 nervous / lacking confidence (no direct opposite)
5 impatient
6 impolite
7 unprofessional

reading

1 D	5 D
2 A	6 B
3 C	7 B
4 A	

listening

Conversation 1
1 John Prince
2 1.2 million
3 first
4 57643467

Conversation 2
5 Head Office
6 production
7 KS145
8 3.15

Conversation 3
9 shipping
10 stock
11 4,250
12 Friday morning

tapescript

Conversation 1

A Kiev supplies, how can I help you?

B This is John Prince calling about an order.

A Sorry, I didn't catch your name.

B It's Prince. P-R-I-N-C-E.

A I've got that. Can you tell me what type of order?

B Sure, it was for 1.2 million pipe brackets!

A Of course, Mr Prince. Let me put you through to Ludmilla – she's dealing with that order … Mr Prince. I'm sorry, I can't get through to her at the moment. Can I take a message?

B Sure you can. We were expecting delivery of the first batch yesterday and there's no sign of them.

A I see. I will get Ludmilla to call you back as soon as she can. Can I just take your telephone number?

B She can reach me on my mobile – that's 075686 5764 3467

A 075686 5764346

B You missed a 7. It's 3467.

A Fine. I've got that. I'll make sure she gets the message. Goodbye.

B Bye.

Conversation 2

C International Pipelines. How can I help you?

D This is Ludmilla Sivorsky from Kiev Supplies Head Office. Can I speak to John Prince?

C I am afraid he's left the office. Have you tried his mobile?

D Yes, I have. I don't think it's switched on. Can I leave a message for him?

C Of course.

D Can you tell him that the first batch of brackets was dispatched yesterday and I cannot understand why he hasn't got them? The driver delivered them to the production site at Kharkov, as requested. I've got a copy of the delivery note – it's KS145 – signed by one of your people at 3.15 yesterday.

C OK. Let me just note that – KS145 at 3.15. It sounds as if there must be a mix-up. I'll try to contact Mr Prince straightaway.

D Thank you. Goodbye.

C Goodbye.

Conversation 3

D Hello. Ludmilla Sivorsky speaking

B Hello, Ludmilla. This is John Prince. I got your message.

D Good. I can't understand why you haven't got the brackets.

B We have and you're quite right – they were delivered to the Kharkov site yesterday. I'm afraid there's been a mistake on our part when the order was processed. We wanted them delivered to Odessa for shipping.

D We had no information about Odessa.

B I know. It's our mistake. What I need to know now is whether you can pick them up and get them down to Odessa, or whether it would be better to transfer another shipment from your central depot.

D We don't have sufficient number in stock to supply them from our depot so we will have to transfer them – but you won't have them for two days minimum.

B Well, we need them as soon as possible. Can you let me know your best delivery time and also the transport costs?

D I can give you the transport costs – just a minute – it will be 4,250 roubles and probably we can get those to you by Friday morning but I will confirm all this in an e-mail.

B Thanks. That would be good. I am sorry about the mix-up.

D No problem. I'll be in contact very soon.

B Thanks, Ludmilla. Goodbye.

D Bye.

language in use

1

1.2 million pipe brackets **were ordered**. Delivery **was expected** on Tuesday 12 June. Unfortunately, the brackets **were delivered** to the wrong location. They **were taken** to the Kharkov site rather than the port at Odessa. A mistake **was made** in filling in the original order form. The brackets **will be picked up** by Kiev Supplies later today. They **will be transported** direct to Odessa. We **are going to be charged** over 4,000 roubles.

2 1 was launched
2 was run
3 were shown
4 visited
5 were reached
6 was distributed
7 launched
8 increased
9 was withdrawn
10 will be / is being prepared
11 anticipate

writing

Model answers

From: orders@truscotts.com
To: h.findale@findale.com
Subject: Delivery Ref No: 200198: 23 x VXE-222

Dear Mr Findale

We tried to deliver the above order earlier today and found the plant closed. Please contact us to advise of a suitable delivery time.

Best regards

Geoff Masters
Customer Services

From: orders@truscotts.com
To: dlong@terrys.com
Subject: Delivery Ref No: 200199: 2 x TPH-16 – damaged in transit

Dear Ms Long

I was sorry to hear about the damage to the TPH-16 in transit. We will arrange for delivery of a replacement tomorrow. I hope this does not cause too much inconvenience.

Best regards

Geoff Masters
Customer Services

fun and games

1 d   4 b
2 a   5 e
3 c

unit 11

vocabulary

1 1 holiday
2 objective
3 encouragement
4 promotion opportunities
5 compensation
6 perks
7 performance reward
8 reduced hours

2 1 maternity leave, sick leave, annual leave, unpaid leave
2 maternity pay, basic pay, pay day, sick pay, annual pay, pay package, full pay
3 working conditions, working day, working hours

3 1 maternity leave; full pay
2 pay package; annual leave
3 sick pay
4 unpaid leave
5 working hours; basic pay
6 working day; working conditions

listening

1 1 H   4 B
2 F   5 D
3 C

2 1 D   4 E
2 G   5 H
3 A

tapescript

1

1 I like my job. I've been here for more than ten years now and I still look forward to going to work every morning. I guess the biggest plus is my colleagues – you know, we all get on so well together. There's a good atmosphere and we all have a laugh. I suppose it's not so secure nowadays, but it's a lot of fun.

2 I suppose I took the job because I knew this type of work wasn't going to go away. You know there are so many jobs in the private sector which are here today and gone tomorrow. But if you work in public health, you know that there are always going to be ill people! It's not just that of course. I like the work as well.

3 What I like about the company is that it's very dynamic – it never stands still. This means for someone of my age there is lots of potential. I could get a job in one of the foreign subsidiaries or I might go to Head Office next. There's a lot of stress – they keep you on your toes, but I like that.

4 When I decided to go back to work, I had to find something which was flexible. I've got two young children and I sometimes need to pick them up after school. The salary's okay but the really great thing is the flexitime system – as long as I'm here between ten and three, I can choose how I make up the rest of my hours.

5 I didn't think I'd stay long but in this line of business there are some great opportunities. It's a great sector to be in – you know, the whole environment. Because we're in sports management, we get a lot of complimentary tickets. This last year I've been to the European Cup Final and The French Open in Paris. Not only that but we get to meet the stars in the hospitality areas as well. I love it.

2

1 They made a big thing about it at the interview. But, to be honest, I'm not sure there's so much advantage. You have to declare the total cost and the tax authorities consider it all as income. The only advantage is that the company can negotiate some very good prices with the manufacturers, so you get it for much less than if you were buying it yourself.

2 It wouldn't be so bad if we got paid for the extra hours but we don't as a rule. Last week I must have done at least 60 hours. My contract demands 39 so I should be getting 21 hours extra pay and some of that was at the weekend so it should be at least time and a half.

3 It's a great time of year to get something extra in your pay packet. If you come from a big family like I do it's expensive getting presents for all the relatives.

4 I wouldn't have taken the job if there wasn't some subsidy to cover travel. The rail tickets have gone up a lot and I would probably be better off taking a job locally. It's bad enough having to commute every day but at least we don't have to pay much.

5 You can't rely just on the state handouts – you'd be very poor come your retirement so I appreciate the contributions the company makes – it should mean that I can retire on 60% of my final salary.

reading

1 B	4 D
2 C	5 D
3 A	6 B

language in use

1 getting
2 Motivating
3 taking
4 covering
5 doing
6 Being; travelling
7 complaining
8 reducing
9 saving
10 sitting; talking

writing

Model answer

> Memo
> To: Management staff
> From: Joe Wild, HR Manager
> Date: 2 June
> Subject: Incentive Scheme
>
> As you all know, **we are planning to introduce a new staff incentive scheme.**
> There are **three options to consider:**
> 1 Christmas bonus
> 2 Performance bonus
> 3 Profits share
> I would be interested to know **what you think about these options.**
> Please **let me have your feedback** by 15 June.

fun and games

1 c, e
2 a, b, f
3 d, g

unit 12

vocabulary

1 1 negotiate
2 win
3 provide
4 request
5 build
6 renew

2 1 d	4 f
2 b	5 e
3 a	6 c

reading

1
01 HAS
02 IN
03 FOR
04 WHICH
05 FINE

06 CORRECT
07 BY
08 CORRECT
09 SEEMS
10 AS
11 CORRECT
12 FOR

2 1 C	6 C	11 B
2 A	7 B	12 A
3 B	8 B	13 B
4 D	9 D	14 C
5 A	10 C	15 B

listening

Conversation 1
1 Flowers
2 Monday
3 ZXY 205
4 876653

Conversation 2
5 BA798
6 16.15
7 B890 UWY
8 departures entrance

Conversation 3
9 Jeanne
10 13 June
11 436
12 6554 2678

tapescript

Conversation 1

A 5-star travel. The office is closed until nine o'clock tomorrow. Please ring back or leave a message after the tone.

B This is Sally Flowers – that's F-L-O-W-E-R-S. I should have received my plane tickets by the beginning of this week. My flight is on Monday. Um the booking reference is ZXW, no I mean ZXY 205. Please call me back as soon as possible and arrange for the tickets to be sent or picked up. My phone number is 09467 876653.

Conversation 2

C ATC Parking. Can I help you?

D I hope so. This is Josh Stanton. I've been waiting at this airport for nearly one hour now. I called you as soon as I got in and I understood you would pick me up in about 15 minutes.

C I'm sorry, sir. There must have been a mix-up. Can I just take some details?

D I've already given those. I just want picking up.

C I understand, sir, but I need to check your details so that we can have your car ready.

D OK. So my flight was BA798 from Singapore and it landed about 16.15. My name's Stanton.

C Fine, I've got that. Can I just have your car type and registration?

D Yes, it's a Renault. A blue Laguna and the registration is B890 UWY.

C Right, sir. I'll get a car to pick you up within ten minutes and we'll have your car waiting.

D Fine, I'll be waiting.

C I was just going to check. Are you by the car hire entrance?

D No. I'm at the departures entrance.

C Fine. We'll pick you up there immediately.

D Thanks. Goodbye.

Conversation 3

E Aircare Baggage Handling. Can I help you?

F Yes, I'm calling on behalf of a client of ours. A Mrs Donovan who arrived at Dublin on a flight from Johannesburg yesterday.

E Right. And there's a problem with her luggage?

F There is. We were told it would be delivered to her hotel last night. It's still hasn't arrived.

E Can I just take a few details?

F Of course.

E So the passenger is Donovan. What's the first name?

F It's Jeanne – J-E-A-N-N-E.

E And she arrived yesterday – the 14th?

F No, the day before.

E OK, the 13th June. And the flight number was?

F Just a moment … um, it was GB 987.

E Thank you. And the luggage tag number?

F It's GB 987 436.

E Right, and you're expecting the case to be dropped off where?

F At the Mercury Hotel in the city centre.

E I wonder if it's gone to the Mermaid. That's happened a few times. I'll check and call you back as soon as I have some news.

F That would be helpful. My name's Jenny and the number is 0278 6554 2678.

E 655 426 … um …

F 78.

E 42678. I'll call you back. Bye.

F Goodbye.

language in use

1 1 If we had travelled first class, we wouldn't have met an old friend in economy.

2 If we hadn't met an old friend in economy, we would have slept on the flight.

3 If we had slept on the flight, we wouldn't have felt so tired when we landed.

4 If we hadn't felt so tired when we landed, we would have got to the car rental more quickly.

5 If we had got to the car rental more quickly, we wouldn't have missed the last available car.

6 If we hadn't missed the last available car, we wouldn't have caught the bus into town.

writing

> Subject: Satisfaction levels
> Month: June
>
> During June, the results were **better** than in May. However, there were still too **many** customers (24%) who were only partly satisfied. Our aim is to reduce this figure **by** 10% (**or** to 14%) by the end of the year.
>
> The 5% figure for dissatisfied customers **was** mainly due to travel delays **which** unfortunately were outside our control.
>
> The major cause of complaint **was** delays. However, if there **had not been** air traffic control problems the level would have been 20. **18** of the hotel complaints were about the Hotel Mercury where they had problems with drains.

fun and games

1 a steak; another steak, cooked properly

2 a holiday; a refund or a free holiday

3 shoes; a refund or another pair of shoes

4 a car; a free repair

5 a freezer; an extended guarantee

unit 13

vocabulary

1 1 employees   4 Customers
2 Suppliers   5 shareholders
3 community   6 banks

2 1 low labour cost; redundancies
2 bribe
3 code of ethics; values
4 support
5 Ethical
6 legislation; toxic

3 1 There have been a lot of redundancies.
2 The employees are not really committed to their jobs.
3 Employees sometimes volunteer in the local community.
4 The company has seconded staff to India.
5 The business community has bribed a lot to get what it wants.
6 This brand of trainers was popular until it was discovered that they were made in sweatshops.
7 Nowadays, job candidates are more interested in a prospective company's code of ethics.
8 Arcon has polluted the River Trask much/considerably less in the last few years.

4 learning tips
1 to draw on / up
2 to opt for
3 to think about / of / up
4 to care about / for
5 to be aware of
6 to depend on
7 to admit to
8 to look forward to

reading

1 C	4 D	7 C
2 B	5 B	
3 A	6 A	

listening

1 B	4 B	7 A
2 C	5 A	8 C
3 B	6 B	

tapescript

A Rosanne, can you start by telling us something about your job?

B Sure. I am head of Corporate Affairs at Zintec. I look after our external communication which means that I make sure the company's corporate message reaches its targets.

A And what are those targets?

B We see them in terms of all the groups and individuals who have a stake in the company. Of course, there's the shareholders – they need to understand why we need their financial support. Then there's the employees – my colleague David

Carter, VP for Internal Communication looks after them – we need to involve them closely in the company's mission.

A I see – and what's the mission?

B Very simple, really. It's to develop treatments which have a significant impact on the health of the world ...

A That's a big mission.

B Yes, it is, but it's one which we need to communicate effectively to all our stakeholders.

A Yes. I'm sorry I interrupted you.

B That's okay. I mentioned the shareholders and the employees. In view of our mission, the most important stakeholder is the end-user of our drugs – in other words, the patients.

A But they don't decide which drugs to take?

B Yes and no. It's true that doctors prescribe the drugs but they have to work for the patients – so the acid test is really them. And nowadays patients are a pretty well-informed group.

A What about the doctors? How do you get them on your side?

B Basically by having the products they are looking for. I mean doctors are primarily interested in curing their patients. If we can help them, they will look to us. So it's our job to educate and inform doctors about the breakthroughs we make.

A Of course. But don't you think there's a thin line between education and entertainment? We hear about the medical conferences in luxury resorts which companies like yours sponsor.

B I think you'll find that's a thing of the past. In many of our markets, medical associations have produced strict guidelines about the sort of hospitality their members can accept.

A So no more lectures in the morning and golf in the afternoon?

B There's very little of that nowadays. Certainly at Zintec, our medical meetings are serious and usually held in the evenings after work.

A What about your relationship with the press? I guess that is also one of your concerns.

B You're right. I also look after our corporate press relations. That means I act as a media spokesperson for the company – you know, regular press conferences.

A Recently the pharmaceutical industry has been getting a bad press for re-

launching drugs with basically the same active substance, in order to prolong patents.

B Yes, that's unfortunate. But I can only speak for Zintec. We have a hard-fought reputation for innovation and we are not going to risk that by launching me-too drugs.

A Well, thank you, Rosanne. That just about covers it.

B You're welcome.

language in use

1 Customer service is vital for all ~~the~~ organisations.
2 We have targeted **the** youth of today as **the** most profitable market.
3 We have introduced **a** code of ethics. This outlines **the** underlying values which all ~~the~~ employees must subscribe to.
4 Our strategy in **the** Third World has been approved by **the** World Health Organisation.
5 We can accept gifts up to the value of $20.
6 In **the** United Kingdom, we give ~~the~~ tips to taxi drivers and hairdressers.
7 A line between **a** tip and **a** bribe is sometimes difficult to draw.
8 In **a** developing country, ~~the~~ petty corruption is probably more visible than in a developed country.
9 Large-scale corruption influences many aspects of ~~the~~ life in this country.
10 ~~A~~ behaviour is different in the country. There is much less corruption than in **a** town.

writing

Model answer

Subject: Ethical issues in the pharmaceutical industry

Findings

This report deals with three main issues which currently concern the industry:

1 Providing solutions for the developing world.
   Critics say that our industry does not invest enough in research to help the Third World.
2 Cost of new drugs.
   We are often accused of not making our products available at reasonable prices.
3 Relationship with the medical profession.
   Some people believe the relationship is too close and that we have too much influence over doctors.

Recommendation
We need to show our critics that we invest heavily in new treatments for major diseases, explain the cost of research and development, and show the world that we support the medical profession but do not have power over it.

unit 14

vocabulary

1 1 g   4 h   7 d
    2 i   5 a   8 e
    3 b   6 c   9 f

2 1 video-conferencing
    2 mobile telephone; fixed line
    3 open-plan offices
    4 typewriter
    5 daily travel to work
    6 Hot-desking
    7 face-to-face meetings
    8 letters
    9 e-mails
    10 Telecommuting

3

adjective	opposite adjective
efficient	inefficient
productive	unproductive
co-operative	unco-operative
accessible	inaccesible
flexible	inflexible
stressful (stressed)	unstressful (stress free / unstressed)
professional	unprofessional
available	unavailable
noisy	quiet
expensive	inexpensive

4 1 inaccessible
    2 expensive / unproductive / inefficient / stressful
    3 co-operation
    4 accessible / available
    5 expensive
    6 unproductive; productive
    7 stress; stressful
    8 flexible; productive / efficient
    9 noisy
    10 unprofessional

reading

1 B   3 F   5 C
2 D   4 E

listening

1 1 C   4 E
    2 H   5 D
    3 F

2 1 D   4 H
    2 G   5 A
    3 C

tapescript

1

1 The biggest change we've had here has been in management. You know, before they were a pretty distant lot – their own canteen. We only saw them when they had something to complain about. Now they're always around.

2 I don't like the new way we have to work. Before you knew where you stood. Now you get in on a Monday morning and you've no idea what you're going to be doing. I often have to answer the phones and check the stock at the same time as dealing with deliveries!

3 My working hours have changed a lot. I used to do very long hours in the office. Now I'm there only a couple of days a week. I'm based at home so now I plan my day to suit myself. I'm on-line with the office so they can contact me any time.

4 Information has gone absolutely mad. I get about 100 e-mails a day. I've to spend most of the morning processing them. A lot of them are irrelevant but I still have to read them before deleting them.

5 We all used to have our own offices. You know big desk. Secretary outside to deal with all the calls and to keep unwanted visitors out. Now we all work in this massive room. It's much more friendly, but sometimes I miss the privacy of my own office.

2

1 I think there'll be more leisure time. You know, we won't need so many workers. Robots and machines will do the work and we'll be able to take it easy.

2 There's likely to be more job insecurity. I expect people will change their job six or seven times in their life and not only for another company or employer but perhaps a complete change of career – you know, computer programmers becoming gardeners!

3 I think we'll all have to work longer – you know, into our seventies. There are going to be too many older people and not enough younger ones to support us. So they're going to have to postpone pensions and make us work longer.

4 We might see a change in the cities. I reckon more and more companies are going to move out – you know, to better, more attractive environments and the cities are going to be left – a bit like museums.

5 I think it'll be developed – you know, we'll find minerals on other planets. There'll be research stations up there and maybe we'll even go for holidays. It's unlikely to be in the next ten years or so but if you look further ahead, I reckon that's the next big frontier.

language in use

1 1 will
    2 should
    3 could / may / might
    4 won't
    5 won't

2 1 expect
    2 won't
    3 doubt
    4 will
    5 could / may / might
    6 could / may / might
    7 'm sure we won't
    8 should

writing

    1 E-mail use
    2 The purpose of this report
    3 Findings
    4 According to the survey
    5 The current situation
    6 This trend is likely to continue
    7 Conclusions
    8 Another concern
    9 Recommendations
   10 We recommend

sample writing tasks

Writing Part 1

1

1 **has** discovered, **ways** of communicating, **suggests**, **are** more careful

2 The question asks the writer to suggest other ways of communicating.

2

1 **would** like, need **you to** confirm, **your** project reports

2 Dear all (or no greeting); Best regards / Regards

3

Note 2 is better.

Note 1
- doesn't mention the meeting
- errors: **I was delayed because I was working** or the time reference (*last night*) needs to be dropped; **Ask our supplier**
- style / content: generally appropriate, but *another lot of* is too colloquial
(Suggested mark: 7/10)

Note 2
- all points covered
- errors: this **afternoon's** meeting; inform **him**
- style / content: excellent and appropriate
(Suggested mark: 9/10)

Writing Part 2

1

Content: all four points covered in an appropriate way.

Organisation: the reason for writing is clearly stated in the opening sentence. Paragraphing and linking devices create a coherent and logical effect.

Format: suitable opening and closing used (Dear Sir – Yours sincerely)

Register: appropriate – generally formal and polite

Target reader: the letter would be very likely to have the required effect on the reader.

NB: some minor grammatical errors which do not impede understanding.

(Suggested mark: 18/20)

2

Content: advertising is not mentioned. Some irrelevant information.

Organisation: the reason for writing is clear. Information is presented clearly and logically.

Format: suitable for a report.

Register: appropriately neutral.

Target reader: all points are reasonably well conveyed.

NB: some minor grammatical errors.

(Suggested mark: 14/20)